The
Workbench
AR-15
Project

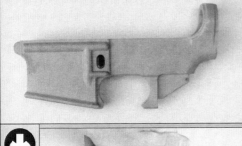

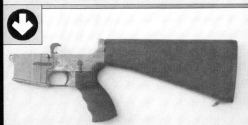

The Workbench AR-15 Project

A Step-by-Step Guide to Building Your Own Legal AR-15 without Paperwork

D.A. Hänks

PALADIN PRESS • BOULDER, COLORADO

The Workbench AR-15 Project:
A Step-by-Step Guide to Building Your Own Legal AR-15
without Paperwork
by D.A. Hänks

Copyright © 2004 by D.A. Hänks

ISBN 13: 978-1-58160-453-5

Printed in the United States of America

Published by Paladin Press, a division of
Paladin Enterprises, Inc.,
Gunbarrel Tech Center
7077 Winchester Circle
Boulder, Colorado 80301 USA
+1.303.443.7250

Direct inquiries and/or orders to the above address.

PALADIN, PALADIN PRESS, and the "horse head" design
are trademarks belonging to Paladin Enterprises and
registered in United States Patent and Trademark Office.

Visit our Web site at www.paladin-press.com

WARNING

Construction or possession of the firearms described in this book may be illegal under federal, state, or local laws. It is the reader's responsibility to research and comply with all applicable laws.

Technical information presented in this book regarding the construction, use, adjustment, and alteration of firearms inevitably reflects the author's individual beliefs and experiences with particular firearms, equipment, tools, and components under specific circumstances that the reader cannot duplicate exactly. The information in this book should therefore be used for guidance only and approached with great caution. Neither the author, publisher, nor distributors of this book assumes any responsibility for the use or misuse of information contained in this book.

This book is for academic study only.

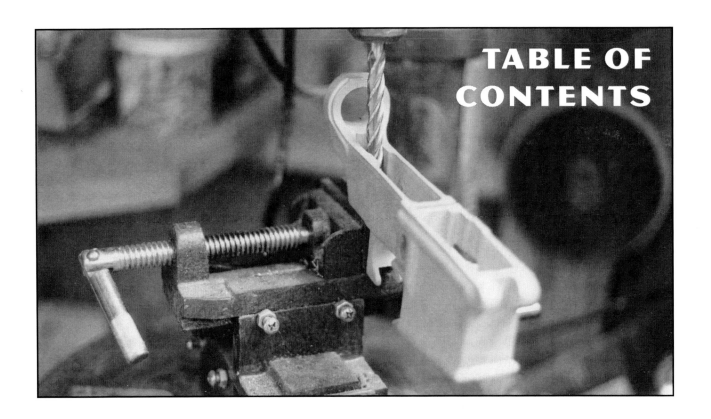

TABLE OF CONTENTS

ACKNOWLEDGMENTS

I would like to thank all of those who believed in me and gave me the encouragement to write this book, my friends and family members, and everyone who still believes law-abiding citizens have the right to keep and bear arms. Most of all, I would like to thank my brother-in-law, Bob. Although he didn't share my passion for firearms, he was my biggest supporter in writing this book. Despite his fighting a losing battle with cancer, he immediately cheered up and congratulated me when I told him of Paladin Press' acceptance of my manuscript. He had always believed in my writing and assured everyone that one day I would become a published author. It is with great sadness that I dedicate this book to his memory. I cannot think of anyone more deserving of my thanks.

In memory of
Robert Charles Goodwin
February 6, 1950—May 14, 2003

LEGAL ISSUES, WARNINGS, AND PLAIN COMMON SENSE

PUBLISHER'S NOTE: *In September 2004, Title XI of the Violent Crime Control and Law Enforcement Act of 1994 (hereafter called the Crime Bill of 1994) was allowed to sunset. Title IX (often referred to as the Assault Weapons Ban because it prohibited the manufacture or importation of certain firearms bearing specific features that the lawmakers considered to be features of assault weapons) was in place when this book was written.*

Paladin decided not to omit the information about the 1994 Crime Bill in this edition, however, because there is a growing movement among gun-control advocates to reenact an assault weapons ban that would contain similar or even more draconian restrictions. Check with the Bureau of Alcohol, Tobacco, Firearms, and Explosives (www.atf.gov) before attempting to manufacture any firearm.

• • •

This book contains no illegal constructions or conversions. It is designed to teach you how to legally build a working AR-15 rifle from an 80 percent finished casting. I will present you with Bureau of Alcohol, Tobacco, and Firearms (BATF, hereafter abbreviated as ATF) and other rules and regulations regarding the construction of homebuilt firearms and assault weapons and legalities thereof.

At the time of this writing, it is completely legal under U.S. Code to build the project in this book as I present it. Any deviation may put you in violation of federal law. Also keep in mind that states such as California have additional restrictions that may bar you from constructing an "assault weapon." It is ultimately up to *you* to check all federal, state, and local laws regarding the construction of a homebuilt, post-ban AR-15 prior to starting this project. I am not an attorney, nor do I profess to have every single answer on these matters. Therefore, *it is your responsibility to ensure that you are not in violation of the law, not mine.* You may direct your questions to the attorney general's office in your respective state and the ATF in Washington, D.C.

In addition, the contents of this book reflect my personal experience with the AR-15 rifle, and none of the steps taken during the course of construction can be exactly duplicated by you, the reader. Therefore, the information contained in this book should be used for guidance only and approached with extreme caution. Neither the author, publisher, nor distributors of this book assumes any responsibility for the use or misuse of any information contained in this book.

The following is a direct cut and paste from the ATF's online FAQ page (italics are mine). You may view this for yourself at http://www.atf.treas.gov/firearms/faq/faq2.htm#a7.

(A7) Does the GCA [Gun Control Act of 1968] prohibit anyone from making a handgun, shotgun or rifle?

> With certain exceptions a firearm may be made by a nonlicensee provided it is not for sale and the maker is not prohibited from possessing firearms. However, *a person is prohibited from making a semiautomatic assault weapon* or *assembling a nonsporting semiautomatic rifle* or nonsporting shotgun from *imported parts.* In addition, the making of an NFA [National Firearms Act of 1934] firearm requires a tax payment and approval by ATF. An application to make a machinegun will not be approved unless documentation is submitted showing that the firearm is being made for a federal or state agency. [18 U. S. C. 922 (o), (r), (v), and 923, 27 CFR 178.39, 178.40, 178.41 and 179.105]

This ruling deals more with AK-47s, FN FALs, and other firearms that are basically constructed from nothing but imported parts. The regulations governing the number of imported parts allowed on an AK-47, for example, seem to be designed more to confuse the average gun owner than anything else.

What this means to you in terms of building an AR-15—being that it is classified as an assault weapon—is this: if you somehow manage to find imported AR-15 parts (I have never seen them offered for sale), *do not use them on this project!* In addition, this project *must* be built as a post-ban rifle—*no exceptions.* (More on pre-ban vs. post-ban below.) If you put pre-ban uppers or collapsible stocks on these lowers, or if you use M16 internal parts, you are in violation of the Violent Crime Control and Law Enforcement Act of 1994 (better known as the 1994 Crime Bill, or the Brady Bill) and subject to a fine not to exceed $10,000 and/or a term of imprisonment not to

exceed 10 years. Intentional violations simply to build a "cool looking" rifle simply are not worth it.

What, then, classifies an otherwise ordinary firearm as an "assault weapon"? Here is the official ATF list at the time of this writing. I have italicized the appropriate sections regarding the AR-15 as it applies to building your own rifle for personal use.

(30) The term "semiautomatic assault weapon" means;

(A) any of the firearms, or copies or duplicates of the firearms in any caliber, known as;

(i) Norinco, Mitchell, and Poly Technologies Avtomat Kalashnikovs (all models);

(ii) Action Arms Israeli Military Industries UZI and Galil;

(iii) Beretta AR70 (SC-70);

(iv) Colt AR-15;

(v) Fabrique National FN/FAL, FN/LAR, and FNC;

(vi) SWD M-10, M-11, M-11/9, and M-12;

(vii) Steyr AUG;

(viii) INTRATEC TEC-9, TEC-DC9 and TEC-22; and

(ix) revolving cylinder shotguns, such as (or similar to) the Street Sweeper and Striker 12;

(B) a semiautomatic rifle that has an ability to accept a detachable magazine and has at least 2 of;

(i) a folding or telescoping stock;

(ii) a pistol grip that protrudes conspicuously beneath the action of the weapon;

(iii) a bayonet mount;

(iv) a flash suppressor or threaded barrel designed to accommodate a flash suppressor; and

(v) a grenade launcher;

(C) a semiautomatic pistol that has an ability to accept a detachable magazine and has at least 2 of;

(i) an ammunition magazine that attaches to the pistol outside of the pistol grip;

(ii) a threaded barrel capable of accepting a barrel extender, flash suppressor, forward handgrip, or silencer;

(iii) a shroud that is attached to, or partially or completely encircles, the barrel and that permits the shooter to hold the firearm with the nontrigger hand without being burned;

(iv) a manufactured weight of 50 ounces or more when the pistol is unloaded; and

(v) a semiautomatic version of an automatic firearm; and

(D) a semiautomatic shotgun that has at least 2 of;
    (i) a folding or telescoping stock;
    (ii) a pistol grip that protrudes conspicuously beneath the action of the weapon;
    (iii) a fixed magazine capacity in excess of 5 rounds; and
    (iv) an ability to accept a detachable magazine.

(31) The term "large capacity ammunition feeding device";

(A) means a magazine, belt, drum, feed strip, or similar device manufactured after the date of enactment of the Violent Crime Control and Law Enforcement Act of 1994; enacted Sept. 13, 1994; that has a capacity of, or that can be readily restored or converted to accept, more than 10 rounds of ammunition; but

(B) does not include an attached tubular device designed to accept, and capable of operating only with, .22 caliber rimfire ammunition.

This means that the AR-15 is classified as an assault weapon because it has a detachable magazine and at least two of the additional evil features listed under 30B, subsections (i) through (iv). Since it is very difficult to shoot an AR-15 without a pistol grip, that pretty much nullifies all other options, although if someone put a thumbhole stock on an AR-15, then theoretically he or she could still use a flash hider. Theories don't always hold up with the ATF, however, so it might be wise to check with them if you'd like to pursue the idea of a thumbhole stock on an AR-15.

Simply put, avoid *all* the italicized parts and you will not be in *any* violation of the law when building your post-ban project gun. That includes the recently popular civilian-version 37mm grenade launchers.

WHO MAY NOT BUILD THEIR OWN FIREARMS?

Anyone who may legally purchase a rifle, shotgun, or handgun may also legally build their own firearms for personal use. Undoubtedly, you have seen the "no legal disabilities" clause on mail-order ammunition sales and the prohibitions listed on the yellow form when you purchase a firearm. These same prohibitions bar you from building your own firearm. Below is an excerpt from Title I of the Gun Control Act of 1968, which prohibits dealers from selling any firearm or ammunition to any person who is:

a. convicted of or under indictment for a felony
b. a fugitive
c. adjudicated as a mental defective or who has been committed to any mental institution
d. addicted to or an unlawful user of marijuana or a stimulant, depressant, or narcotic drug
e. less than 18 years of age for the purchase of a shotgun or rifle
f. less than 21 years of age for the purchase of a firearm that is other than a shotgun or rifle
g. a nonresident of the state in which the licensee's place of business is located
h. an alien illegally or unlawfully in the U.S.
i. dishonorably discharged from the armed forces
j. subject to a court order that restrains such person from harassing, stalking, or threatening an intimate partner
k. convicted in any court of a misdemeanor crime of domestic violence

With the exception of (f), all rules also apply to anyone wishing to make a homebuilt rifle or shotgun. If the homebuilt firearm is a pistol, then (f) applies as well.

Additional State Laws Regarding Homebuilt Firearms

Your particular state, county, or town may impose additional restrictions or outright bans on certain firearms (homebuilt or not). California and Connecticut, for example, have banned assault weapons. Respective designations vary, so even a post-ban gun may not be legal in some parts of the country. In addition, virtually all firearms are illegal for civilians to own or possess in New York City and Washington, D.C. Again, use common sense, and contact your local law enforcement agency or state attorney general's office if you have any doubts whatsoever about what is legal and illegal when it comes to AR-15s, assault weapons, homebuilt firearms, and firearm ownership and possession.

SERIAL NUMBERS OR OTHER IDENTIFICATION ON THE RECEIVER

The ATF does not *require* a serial number or

any other identifying markings on the receiver of a homebuilt firearm, although they strongly *recommend* one. Interestingly, this does not appear to be for the purpose of identifying the owner but rather for the identification of the firearm itself in case of theft.

The common misconception is that you need to put your name, address, and Social Security number on the receiver. This is simply not the case. Serial numbers are required for licensed manufacturers only. The home-builder is exempt from this because his or her firearms can *never be sold, traded, or even given away* to family or friends, although your spouse may inherit them. After that, they must be destroyed.

If you choose to mark the receiver in some way, you might consider putting it under the pistol grip rather than in plain view on the side of the magazine well. You might choose to stamp or engrave a word, shape, or number on the receiver. Some people put their name, although I personally would *never* do that. A unique steel stamp, such as an oak leaf, will also suffice (maybe with a number or letter). A date of manufacture might be wise. Many people might to choose to ignore this step altogether since it isn't required.

ADDITIONAL RULES REGARDING THE AR-15

Since the vast majority of people undertaking this project are most likely already AR-15 enthusiasts, they probably already have one or two factory-built rifles. There are some very important things you must be aware of, however. The first and foremost subject nowadays is, "What exactly is the difference between a pre-ban and post-ban AR-15?"

Pre-Ban vs. Post-Ban

On September 14, 1994, a day which will live in infamy for gun owners, the Violent Crime Control and Law Enforcement Act went into effect. More commonly known as the 1994 Crime Bill, or the Brady Bill, it effectively changed the status of dozens of rifles, shotguns, and handguns, possibly forever. It created two versions of the same weapon: pre-ban and post-ban.

The designation of pre-ban is as follows: "Any receiver that was *assembled* as a rifle on or before September 13, 1994" is considered to be a pre-

ban. Note that I have italicized the word "assembled." This is where a great deal of confusion arises.

Let's say you have a rifle that was assembled in August of 1994. That is clearly a pre-ban rifle. Now, let's say that the *receiver* was manufactured in August but wasn't assembled into a rifle until the day after the ban went into effect. That is a post-ban rifle! The date of manufacture of the receiver is irrelevant.

Here's another scenario: you buy a lower that was assembled into a rifle before the ban but stripped down again. Is this receiver pre-ban? Yes, because even though it is now a simple receiver, it was at one time actually a rifle and can be restored to its former status.

Now, say you buy a pre-ban lower at a gun show that has obviously never been anything but a stripped lower. Can you use it to build a pre-ban AR-15? No! It was never a rifle. That means unless you can prove that the pre-ban lower (with certified date of manufacture) was assembled into a rifle before the ban, it is technically considered to be post-ban!

What good is an unassembled pre-ban receiver then? There are two reasons. First, proving when it was assembled is a very gray area. According to U.S. law, the burden of proof lies with the prosecution, although I'm sure the ATF would be happy to settle for mere confiscation of the rifle. It would be up to you to take them to court over it, and the expense would override the time and money you had invested in it. Second, you can only build an AR-15 "assault pistol" from a pre-ban lower *that was never assembled into a rifle.*

AR-15 Pistols

Any AR-15 pistol must be built from a "virgin" lower, but post-ban versions cannot be of assault weapon configuration. Bolt, pump-action, or single-shot uppers are still acceptable, as would be a lower with a permanently fixed 5- or 10-round magazine, as long as you build the pistol from a lower that has never been assembled into a rifle.

In addition, there is the "50 ounce rule." Looking back at the ATF's assault pistol designations, one finds that an AR-15 pistol would be in violation because it has a detachable magazine, pistol grip, barrel shroud, and weighs more than 50 ounces with an empty magazine in place. If you took the time to drill a lot of holes in a lower receiver; had a short, lightweight pistol barrel with no semblance of a handguard and no handguard locking rings; and managed to come in at 50 ounces or less, then technically you would not be in possession of an assault pistol.

I would not recommend this for a number of reasons. Your scale might be off. Short-barreled 5.56mm actions do not work properly because there is not enough space between the gas port and muzzle to allow the gas-powered design to work properly. You would also suffer from a severe lack of velocity from the overly short barrel (not to mention excessive muzzle flash). A 9mm upper would work fine with a short barrel because it works on a blowback design rather than utilizing exhaust gases to operate the bolt. Uppers chambered for 9mm are generally heavy barreled, however, so the weight would still be a problem with regards to the 50 ounce rule.

What, then, to do with that 5.56mm, 11½ inch upper you bought? Well never, under *any* circumstances, mount it on your rifle! It then constitutes a short-barreled rifle, which is a violation of the National Firearms Act of 1934 (also known as an "NFA violation"). If you *must* use it, you can purchase a 5½ inch flash hider, but it must be welded or silver-soldered on with 1,100 degree solder to make it permanent. It must also go onto a pre-ban weapon because of the flash hider. You would then have the look of a standard 16½ inch carbine barrel but with significantly reduced muzzle velocity and accuracy. Therefore, the best thing to do is to sell or trade it to a Class 3 dealer who can use it for an XM177 configuration carbine, or sell it to an individual who already has a legal pistol lower to use it on.

Crime Bill Sunset Clause

The part of the 1994 Crime Bill that bans "assault weapons" will sunset in September 2004. If this comes to pass (absolutely no guarantee that it will), the designations pre- and post-ban will become moot. Once again, there will be no restrictions on how you build your AR-15 except for NFA rules regarding short barrels, certain M16 parts, and so forth.

Apparently our legislators weren't convinced that more stringent gun laws would work (and they haven't), so they didn't want it made permanent until it was proven to be a deterrent to crime (which it hasn't). These laws were never intended to curb crime, as criminals will never abide by the law anyway. The 1994 Crime Bill has been a dramatic failure at stopping crime but a tremendous success in further eroding our Constitutional rights.

If the assault weapons ban is voted back in, perhaps even more stringent rules will then become law, thereby destroying even more of our rights to keep and bear arms. Let your representatives in Congress know your views, and remind them that they are in office to serve *your* best interests, not theirs!

"A well regulated Militia, being necessary to the security of a free State, the right of the people to keep and bear Arms, shall not be infringed."
Amendment II, United States Constitution

INTRODUCTION

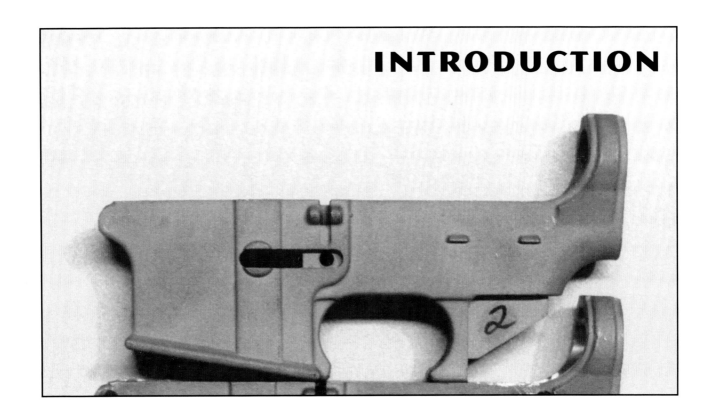

---

*It is suggested that you read this book in its entirety
before attempting this project.*

The AR-15 rifle is without a doubt the most versatile firearm ever designed. The basic design of a barreled upper receiver separate from the lower receiver naturally makes the substitution of different uppers a virtual plethora of possibilities for the shooter or enthusiast. It allows the shooter to have one lower receiver and several uppers to suit a variety of needs, essentially creating several rifles from one.

Upper receivers are available in calibers ranging from .22 LR all the way to .50 BMG. This means that one AR-15 can be configured into a full-length rifle that can plink tin cans off a fence or take down a Cape buffalo at 1,500 yards. If you prefer shorter guns, that same AR-15 can be made into a carbine or even a pistol.

With the introduction of the Brady Bill in 1994, we were suddenly faced with the designation of "pre-ban" and "post-ban" configurations of so-called assault weapons. This has left the general public with a great degree of uncertainty when it comes to AR-15s, so a quick review of the legal terrain is in order.

Any lower receiver that you build yourself now automatically falls under the post-ban designation and must be assembled in accordance with federal law. Simply put, this means you cannot have a collapsible stock, flash hider, or bayonet lug on your AR-15. If you use a post-ban upper and an A1, A2, or *fixed* M4-style stock, you will be all set. I know of no imported AR-15 parts, so that is not an area to be concerned with, *but you must have no M16 internal parts in a post-ban AR-15!* This includes the bolt carrier! You may still use pre-ban, high-capacity magazines in your post-ban weapon, however.

As long as you follow a *commercial* firearm design (zip guns or other improvised firearms are illegal because they are not of a professionally engineered design) and suffer from no legal restrictions, you may legally build firearms for personal use. A commercially designed firearm constitutes a design that has been engineered, tested, and produced by a commercial manufacturer. As far as I know, there is no record of a *legally* homebuilt firearm having ever been used in a crime.

Finally, your homebuilt firearm cannot be sold, traded, or legally passed on to your children (although your spouse may retain it).

If you are still intrigued by the thought of building a real, working firearm that will actually fire ammunition safely upon completion, then I have just the project for you! By finishing your own lower receiver, you not only have the option to put a custom upper on it, you also will save a *lot* of money. Complete post-ban AR-15s in .223 or 5.56mm are selling for $600 to $800, but I have built one from a casting for as little as $400! That was with a basic pistol grip and used stock and getting a law-enforcement discount on the internal parts, but you see the possibilities. New or camouflaged stocks and custom grips will add to the cost of the weapon, as will out-of-the-ordinary caliber uppers such as 9mm, 7.62mm, .45 ACP, or .300 Whisper. But you can still build a basic, *non-standard*-caliber AR-15 for around $650 compared to $750–$2,500 for a commercial version, depending on caliber and whether it is pre-ban or post-ban. Most manufacturers/builders of these other-calibered rifles have stopped doing so and are selling the uppers only, which are very plentiful, so you still save by making your own lower as opposed to paying for it.

A few companies offer for sale partially finished castings and forgings of AR-15 lower receivers. These range in completion from 50 to 80 percent, the legal limit without involving paperwork.

Paperwork! Ah, the magic word! With the Gun Violence Prevention Act of 1998 (Brady 2) now in implementation, any firearm purchase is recorded by the FBI unless you are fortunate enough to live in a state where a pistol permit or a concealed-carry permit negates the federal background check. But many people do not agree with the notion of having to file paperwork with the government in order to possess a firearm. Some think that such paperwork can and will be used to confiscate guns from law-abiding citizens (and there is ample historical precedent for this,

from Communist China to Nazi Germany). Others simply feel it is a gross violation of every American citizen's Second Amendment rights. In any case, a way around the paperwork involved in the purchase of a complete AR-15 or a factory lower from which to build your own rifle from parts is to get a partially finished casting and complete it yourself.

Recently there has been talk at the ATF to reclassify these castings to require paperwork for them. This is mostly due to people who, quite frankly, know nothing of what they are talking about. They are convinced that these castings are so simple to finish that they qualify as complete lowers. This is ludicrous, but it shows the mentality of those who seek to regulate them because they are misinformed as to the degree of difficulty in finishing them. These are the same people who view gun shows as places where terrorists and Third World armies equip themselves with everything from small arms to Stinger missiles. Their hysteria and ignorance would be almost laughable if the consequences to law-abiding gun owners weren't so dire.

To some this process may appear deceptively easy, but *it is not that simple.* You cannot merely acquire the casting, drill a few holes in it, drop an upper receiver onto it, and be ready to go. If you are expecting to simply assemble some parts in an hour or so, you are very much mistaken. While it does not require a degree in rocket science to accomplish, it is not a two-hour project either. Expect to spend at least eight hours *minimum* if you have a jig and at least a full weekend if you are using a different method. Your first project will most likely take you a week or two to complete. If you can only work on it after hours (most of us have full-time jobs), it may take you a few weeks or more.

However, the rewards are well worth the time, and once you are familiar with the process, things will speed up. For those with no experience in this type of project, fear not. This book will guide you through it step by step, with detailed photographs and instructions. Upon completion, you will have a rifle that you will be proud to shoot or display and be able to say, "I made this!"

I do not have a machine shop. In fact, I have no metalworking equipment at all. All my receivers are completed in my little wood shop. I have a large drill press that I have equipped with a multidirectional vise, but aside from that (and the cobalt drill bits if you use them), all the tools for this project can be used on wood. Therefore, anyone with a home workshop can finish these receivers with relatively few tools. With a jig it becomes even easier, but again, do not expect to complete this project in less than eight hours. Allow yourself at least a weekend to enjoy the work and immerse yourself in some quality "gun time."

A few companies offer not only these castings but also partially complete forgings for sale as more and more people are discovering this popular new market. Now is the time to get one or more lowers while they are still readily available. They are fairly inexpensive, so you can even stock up on them now to build your AR project later in the event of any new ATF rulings on the sale of castings.

I use lowers from The Tannery Shop exclusively because they are investment castings meant to be sold to commercial manufacturers. They are of extremely good quality and have the full 80 percent work cast into them. Some of the others for sale have a different method to the casting and not as much work done on them. The makeup of the metal also appears to be different. Therefore, I will be using a Tannery Shop lower for this project, although I list other sources at the end of the book. You can locate still more sources for these castings via the Internet.

These lower castings have been available in aluminum since the 1980s, but in more recent years they have become available in other metals and alloys. The wave of new materials hit the market in 1998, although some were available prior to the 1994 Crime Bill. The castings are currently available in heat-treated 356 (T6) aluminum, ceramic matrix metal (CMM), copper/beryllium, aluminum/bronze, 410 stainless steel, and, for those with access to some really good tools, titanium.

So which lower is best? Well, that depends upon your specific needs. Therefore, the question should be which lower is best for you. I need to point out that there is no machining done to these lowers; all the work is *cast* into them, not machined out (except in the case of the milled forgings, of course). It looks machined because it appears that material has been removed, when in fact it was never there because the voids (mag well, fire-control pocket, etc.) have been cast into the lower.

For a first-time project or if you wish to build only one rifle, I strongly recommend the copper/beryllium casting (henceforth referred to as a bronzie) for several reasons. First, it has the most work done to it. The top plane (the area where the upper receiver mates with the lower) requires no milling and, although undersized, the rear takedown hole is already cast in the exact location; it only needs enlarging. This is particularly useful if you are using another lower for a jig. Another important feature of a bronzie lower is that if you do drill a hole in the wrong location, you can tap the hole and thread a piece of brass rod to make a plug. Solder the plug in place and you are back in business.

The only working drawback to the bronzie is that the alloy is rather hard and if you aren't careful, your drill bits can wander and you may end up with misaligned holes. I chose the bronzie for my first AR project and did in fact have one hole (out of 15) that was $\frac{1}{64}$ of an inch too low and to the front. This was rectified with the aforementioned brass rod and solder. After a little filing it was as good as new.

The bronzie lower weighs approximately three pounds and is more suitable for a target rifle or a .50 BMG upper. With the additional weight, however, recoil was almost nonexistent on the carbine configuration when I test-fired it, and there was zero muzzle climb. I used one for my 7.62x39mm upper because, out of all the AR-15 upper configurations I own, it is the round with the heaviest recoil other than the .50 BMG.

One drawback to all the lowers (other than aluminum or CMM) is the price. Titanium, for example, will run you three and a half times the cost of a T6 lower. For specific applications, however, they may be worth the extra price. At the time of publication, T6 was running $80; CMM $95; 410 stainless, copper/beryllium, and bronze/aluminum (also known as a brassy) $175; and titanium a whopping $275. You can get factory seconds for substantial savings from time to time, which may have a few blemishes or tighter tolerances in the magazine wells. I recently purchased T6 seconds for $45 apiece! I will be demonstrating the projects in this book on some of these very seconds, and I will deliberately screw one up to show you various methods for correcting mistakes. These seconds are easily identifiable in the photos by the number 2 on the pistol grip web.

The T6 aluminum lowers are by far the most popular castings to use because they are light-weight, easy to work, and the cheapest. T6 is also the traditional material for the AR-15. If you make a mistake in your aluminum lower, it is a little more difficult to correct the problem than on a bronzie or brassy (which can be soldered), but all is not lost. You can fill the hole with cold-weld epoxy and redrill, although I'm not sure of the long-term durability of epoxy for holding your spring-tensioned pins in place. Another method is to fill the hole with the aluminum soldering rods you can usually find for sale at car shows, swap meets, or flea markets. This is a superior method for filling an improperly drilled hole, but it might anneal the temper of the heat-treated aluminum casting. Since at least one commercial AR-15 manufacturer is now selling *plastic* lowers, I don't see how this would be a major problem with regard to the performance of the weapon.

CMM is very similar to aluminum except that it is a little stronger and therefore a few dollars more to purchase. It machines in the same manner, although when using a file to dress your top plane, the tiny particles of ceramic tend to catch in the file and make annoying gouges in your surface.

Aluminum/bronze will make a beautiful AR-15 lower if you polish it, as it looks identical to brass. It is also known as marine brass in some parts of the country because it is extremely corrosion resistant, making it ideal for exposure to marine elements.

Stainless steel is a very tough metal, although not as hard as one would think. A stainless lower has merit for building a shiny, stainless, bull-barreled target rifle or for additional strength when building a .50 BMG rifle.

Titanium is very strong, hard, and lightweight. It would be the ideal material for a .50 BMG upper because of the additional strength it would provide to absorb the power of that round without adding weight to the gun, but the extreme difficulty in milling and machining it does not warrant the aggravation involved for most people. It should be used by advanced or experienced builders only; it's definitely not for the novice.

T6 lowers are now available with the trigger guard cast in place. Buying one saves the additional work of drilling the holes for a standard

guard as well as alleviating the risk of breaking one of the "ears" off during the drilling process. T6 lowers with trigger guards in place cost only a few dollars more.

Standard T6 castings are available that have been precoated with a hard anodized finish. I would recommend using these only with the aid of a drilling jig, and only after you have become proficient with it. (The anodizing is very thin, so it is possible to *carefully* remove it with a miniature grinder at the exact spot you will drill to prevent the bit from wandering.)

In the future, the 80 percent milled forgings may become more available, possibly even replacing the cast lowers because they are superior in quality. They are stronger, and the top plane and fire-control pocket are machined to specification, eliminating these steps from the finishing process. (The fire-control pocket is the space behind the magazine well that extends to the buffer tube hole and contains the hammer, trigger, disconnector, and selector.) At the time of this writing, however, the castings are still more common, so I will refer to the project in this book as "casting" since that is what I used for all the lowers pictured herein.

I will use aluminum castings for the projects in this book, as they are most likely what you will be using for your own project. I will show you two methods for drilling your holes. One involves using an existing AR-15 lower as a jig, the other a commercial drilling jig that, used properly, is virtually idiot-proof.

A commercial jig is by far the best way to achieve a quality lower, although I have made several without one. I cover both processes because you may not want to invest $225 to $600 in a drilling jig for only one or two rifles, although you can always use it for other tasks, rent it to friends, or sell it after your projects are completed. I prefer the OSI Super Jig because it is well made and is designed to be used with the Tannery Shop lowers.

Undoubtedly, many of you (me included) have purchased a 0 percent-finished forging blank at some time or another thinking, "Cool, I can mill this thing out no problem," only to face an almost impossible task. Mine still sits, three years later, on a dusty shelf out in the workshop. The most difficult parts of the lower receiver to mill out are the magazine well and the magazine release area. Fortunately, these areas have been cast into the lowers used in this book, as has the fire-control pocket and an undersized hole for the buffer tube.

What, then, is required of the do-it-yourselfer who wishes to complete one of these castings into a working lower ready to pin onto an upper receiver? Here's what you will need to do:

1) File out the magazine well.
2) Remove some material from the top plane. How much material depends upon fluctuations in the castings, although it generally ranges from almost nothing to $/_{16}$ of an inch.
3) Enlarge the buffer tube hole and tap it.
4) Drill all the other holes that are present in a commercial lower, although a few can be left out if you feel they are too difficult to drill with your particular tools.
5) Slightly enlarge the areas in the fire-control pocket where the rear lug of the upper receiver fits and where the individual fire-control parts fit. This area tends to shrink inward during cooling of the metal after casting.

The mandatory holes are for the trigger and hammer pin, selector (the technical term for the safety lever; I am *not* referring to a select-fire lever), pivot pin, takedown pin, buffer detent, pistol grip screw (which will also need to be tapped), and selector detent. In addition, a shallow hole will need to be drilled in the rear of the receiver to seat the anti-twist nub of the stock.

Optional holes are for the pivot pin detent, takedown pin detent, bolt hold-open spring and pivot pin, and trigger guard. I will explain as we go along what each of these holes is for and why you may or may not want to attempt drilling them. Remember, the fewer holes you have to drill, the less chance of making a mistake!

Most of these optional holes are for when you are completing your casting without the use of a drilling jig. With the aid of a jig, all holes are easily drilled without fear of mistakes, with the exception of the trigger guard holes. I never put trigger guards on any of my rifles anyway, as the step is, to me, unnecessary. The trigger is far enough inside the "ears" of the casting that you cannot damage the trigger if you happen to drop the rifle, and if you want to shoot with gloves or trigger mittens, you do not need to worry about trying to unhinge the guard.

Does this sound like a lot of work? It is . . . and it isn't. Some of it is rather tedious, especially when fitting close tolerances like your top plane and magazine well. This can be rather time consuming, although not necessarily difficult. As long as you take your time and don't rush, you should be fine. The most difficult parts of the process are tapping the buffer hole evenly and locating the holes for your fire-control parts correctly. If your buffer tube hole is tapped out of alignment, your bolt carrier will stick or not recess all the way into the buffer tube. If your fire-control holes do not match evenly from side to side, your fire-control pins will be crooked and the hammer, trigger, or selector will not function properly. Also, if your trigger/hammer pins are aligned evenly but positioned off by just a few thousandths of an inch, it can affect the function of the rifle.

For example, if your hammer is a little too close to the trigger (or vice-versa), it will cock but never release. You would have to grind the front of the trigger down to work properly, and the rifle would never be "to spec" if you wanted to change parts for some reason. The modified trigger would also be useless in another rifle because it would be too short. I had this very scenario happen to me on one particular lower, so I trimmed the trigger down and used that lower for my .50 BMG upper.

If the hammer is closer still to the trigger, it will bind and not move at all. If it is too far away, it will not engage the notch in the sear to cock at all. This will result in a very dangerous (and highly illegal, although spectacular) slam fire that can blow the gun up in your face or get you 10 years in a federal prison and a $10,000 fine. If your selector is too close to the trigger, it can be difficult or even impossible to turn, rendering it useless.

As long as you take your time and don't get too excited to finish the project, you should be fine. Hurrying will only cause you to make mistakes, resulting in lost time to correct the problem(s). Remember, you can always remove more material if need be, but once it's gone, it can't be replaced without a great deal of difficulty, and it's never quite as good as it was before you filed it off or drilled it out. In regards to overfiling, know that if you take too much off the top plane, you have ruined your casting and now have an expensive paperweight. Patience is a virtue and will reward you with many hours of shooting pleasure, so don't get ahead of yourself.

To sum up, this project will require a basic working knowledge of the AR-15 rifle, some mechanical inclination, and access to some tools. If you have a small workshop, then you can complete this project fairly easily if you follow the instructions. If you are attempting this project without the use of a drilling jig, then you will need another AR-15 lower to use for a jig. If you are not familiar enough with the AR-15 to own one, then you should not attempt this project without the aid of a drilling fixture.

Still interested? Good! If I haven't scared you away yet, then grab your eye and ear protection and let's head out to the workshop (or coffee table, as is often the case with me) and get started on finishing your very own 80 percent lower receiver into a working AR-15 rifle that you can be proud of for many years to come.

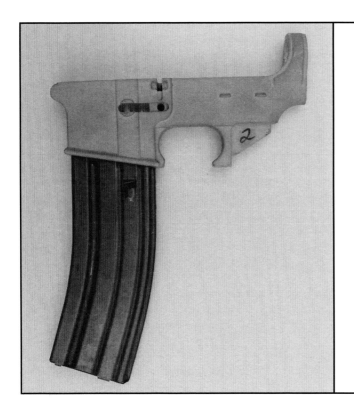

First and foremost, *always wear eye and ear protection* when using power tools. Ear protection will protect you from the noise, and eye protection will protect you from flying shavings, chips, and dust. Eye protection is particularly imperative if you are working with a copper/beryllium or aluminum/bronze casting. Copper particles (bronze and brass are copper based) in your eye can cause blindness if not removed within 24 hours. Beryllium dust is also extremely toxic if inhaled, so wear a particle mask when milling a copper/beryllium casting.

Several parts in this project are held under pressure by springs, some quite strong, so wear your eye protection during assembly/disassembly of parts as well. I once had a hammer slip out and fly up, striking me low on the forehead hard enough to stun me. Luckily the cut was between my eyes, not in one, which could have blinded me had the sharp edge contacted my cornea. The end of the spring could very easily have punctured my eye.

TOOLS AND EQUIPMENT

Here is a list of tools and equipment that you should have to accomplish the task at hand. You may not need all of these items, but I will cover all bases.

Power Tools

- Overhead milling machine or drill press
- Variable-speed hand drill
- A good drill index, preferably with cobalt bits. This is especially true if you will be drilling an alloy harder than aluminum or CMM.
- Rotary file
- 1 inch and $\frac{5}{8}$ inch sanding drums

Hand Tools

- A good assortment of files, including narrow and wide; coarse and smooth; and triangular, half-round, and rattail.
- Scratch awl
- Center punch
- Tap and die set
- $1\frac{3}{16}$ inch x 16 TPI starter tap for the buffer tube hole
- $\frac{15}{16}$ inch or 23mm socket and ratchet to turn the tap if you don't have a tap handle large enough to accommodate a $\frac{1}{2}$ inch tap end
- Very coarse (60) sandpaper
- $\frac{1}{2}$ grit floor-sanding paper
- Duct tape
- Hammer
- Set of punches for removing pins

AR-15 vs. M16 PARTS

I will show the parts for an AR-15 alongside their M16 counterparts so there is no mistaking which part is which. I am comparing the two only so you don't mistakenly put an M16 part in your rifle and violate federal laws.

Let's start with the bolt carrier (Fig. 1), as it's the largest of the parts and easiest to differentiate. Basically, the M16 carrier has more meat on the rear; this is to engage the sear when the rifle is cycled on a select-fire weapon. I will not explain how this works or why, although I know full well, because it has nothing to do with this project. You want an AR-15 bolt carrier on your post-ban project rifle, so make sure it looks like the one on the right.

Next we'll examine the hammers (Fig. 2). The M16 hammer on the right has a small spur on the

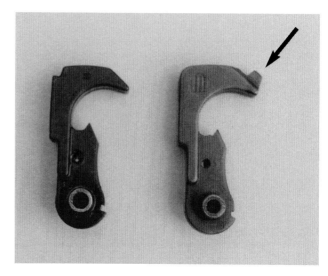

Figure 2. The AR-15 hammer is on the left. The M16 hammer, with its characteristic "spur," is on the right.

back that engages the sear when the rifle is cocked. Again, make sure that yours looks like the one on the left.

From the side both triggers look identical (Fig. 3), but upon closer examination (Fig. 4) we find that the M16 trigger on the right has the groove machined all the way through the back, whereas the AR-15 trigger stops short, creating a closed end. Your trigger needs this solid, closed end.

The disconnectors (Fig. 5) are quite easy to tell apart. The M16 disconnector on the right has a "tail" that fits into the groove of the trigger as well as the fin on the selector. Your disconnector had better not have a tail.

The final part for comparison is the selector (Fig. 6). They are fairly easy to tell apart because

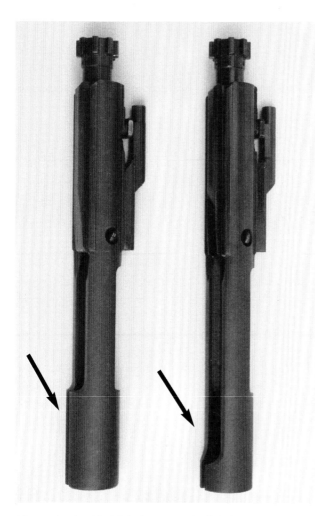

Figure 1. An AR-15 bolt carrier (right) shown next to an M16 bolt carrier (left). Compare the amount of metal where the arrows are pointing

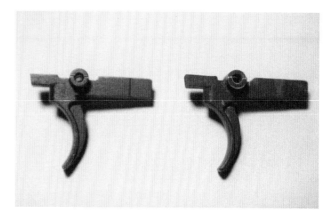

Figure 3. The AR-15 trigger is on the left and the M16 is on the right, although it is impossible to tell from this angle.

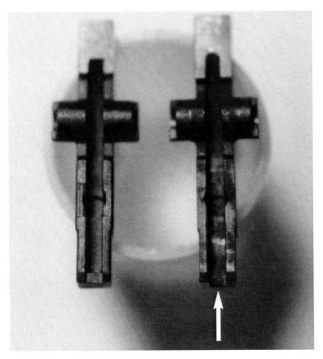

Figure 4. Here we can see that the AR-15 trigger on the left does not have the groove machined all the way to the back as does the M16 trigger on the right.

the AR-15 version is rather plain, whereas the M16 selector has an extra detent divot for the auto position, a fin on the flat surface to disengage the disconnector, and a groove near the selector lever to keep the auto position from becoming a secondary safe position. If you install an M16

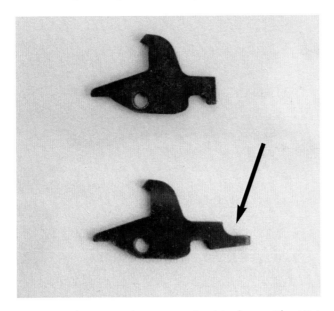

Figure 5. The AR-15 disconnector (top) is shorter. The M16 disconnector (bottom) has the additional "tail."

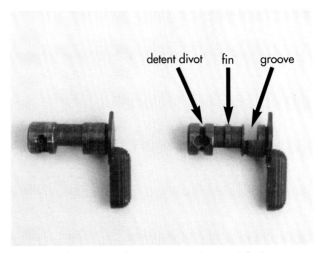

Figure 6. The AR-15 selector is pictured on the left, the M16 on the right. Note the additional machining on the M16 selector.

selector on a rifle with all other AR-15 parts, it will rotate to the auto position but will in fact become a second safety; the trigger will not pull. Again, be certain that your selector matches the one on the left of Figure 6 for the project in this book.

HOW TO FIX A MISTAKE

If you accidentally oversize a hole or drill one in the wrong place, there are a few ways to fix the problem. If your casting is made of a copper-based alloy such as aluminum/bronze or copper/beryllium, you can simply tap the hole, thread a piece of brass or copper rod, and solder it in place. File both sides and you are as good as new.

If you are using an aluminum casting, which is most likely the case, it will be a little trickier, but there are a few options. One is with cold weld, a thick, quick-setting epoxy that can be machined after it cures. There are various brands of cold weld, and you can find it in any auto parts supply store.

As promised, I have deliberately drilled a few holes incorrectly in an aluminum casting to simulate a mistake you might make. Follow the directions to mix the epoxy and apply it to the affected area. It may take a few applications to build it up enough to file down and redrill. In Figure 7, you can see where I have laid the dimension for the selector hole from the top instead of the bottom and fixed it with cold weld. Rather than fill the entire hole and redrill a new one, I used the rotary file to elongate the hole to the correct location, then built up the area where I had drilled first with epoxy (at the arrow). I then carefully filed the epoxy build-up with a rattail file to make its edge curve to fit the hole. For a smaller hole, such as for the hammer or trigger pin, you might be better off filling the entire hole and redrilling. Be careful, though! The epoxy is softer than the metal, and the bit can easily wander into the original hole again.

The second way to fix a mistake—and probably the best way in terms of permanence—is to fill the area with an aluminum soldering rod. These rods can be found at car shows and flea markets. Solder will actually bond metal to the casting (an epoxy adhesive only joins the two), but it can be quite tricky to learn to use. You might have a problem getting the casting hot enough to melt the solder, and you might anneal the tempered casting in the process. Once you get the hang of it, though, you can actually solder across a hole in a soda can without melting it.

The third way is a hybrid of the first and second methods. Tap the hole, thread a piece of aluminum rod, and epoxy it in place. Then file both sides of the plug and simply redrill your hole in the proper location.

The most crucial hole in the project is also the easiest to remedy if you drill it incorrectly. The pivot hole absorbs a lot of stress, and therefore a buildup of epoxy to correct a misaligned hole might not hold up. The answer lies in a little part that was developed to allow older, large-hole ($\frac{1}{4}$ inch) Colt AR-15 lowers to accommodate newer, mil-spec uppers.

When the AR-15 was first introduced to the civilian population, Colt did not want M16 military parts to be readily swapped with those on the civilian AR-15. One of the ways Colt tried to prevent this was to enlarge the pivot pin and holes in the AR-15 receivers. When all the other manufacturers began making AR-15s to military specifications, the point became moot. What, then, to do with your older-model lower to allow it to accept a mil-spec upper?

The answer is an offset pin (Fig. 8). The male portion of the pin inserts from one side and is threaded into the female portion on the other end (Fig. 9). These pins are available from gun parts suppliers like Brownells, Bushmaster, and most AR-15 vendors at gun shows.

This little pin might just save your project if you happen to drill your pivot hole slightly off. If

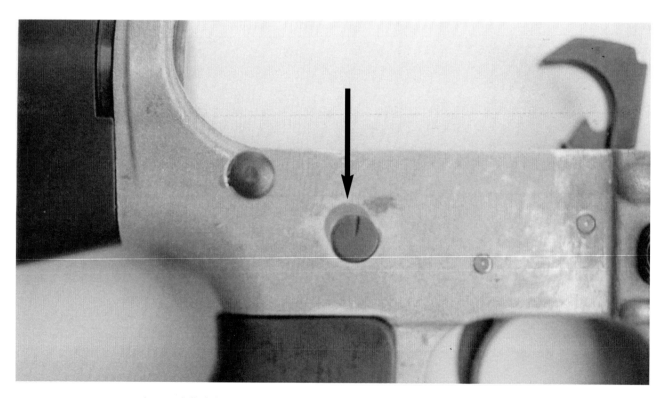

Figure 7. Here we see where I drilled the selector hole in the wrong location and filled it with cold-weld epoxy. So far it has survived 500 rounds fired through the completed rifle with no ill effects.

Figure 8. The conversion offset pin to allow a Colt lower to be joined with a mil-spec upper.

Figure 9. The two parts opened up.

Figure 10. Enlarge the hole accordingly until the stud is centered (arrow).

Figure 11. This what your corrected pivot hole/pin should look like.

the hole is off a smidgen on one side of the lower, you can use a rotary file to get it in the right location, but if it is off considerably (1 millimeter/ 0.04 inch or more on each side), you have a serious problem. Here is where an offset pin will salvage an otherwise ruined receiver. This method will require quite a bit of careful fitting with a rotary file, but it *does* work. (If your pivot hole is off by more than $\frac{1}{16}$ inch, you can trash the casting because even this method won't save you unless you can fill the hole with solder.)

Using the rotary file, elongate the hole until it is positioned where it should be. Next, carefully enlarge this elongated hole to make it perfectly round. Test the size of the hole frequently with the wide center portion of the male end of the offset pin to ensure a snug fit. Don't make the hole too big!

Once the male portion of the pin fits neatly into the hole and holds the upper receiver in place, turn the rifle over and inspect the threaded portion of the pin in relation to the hole on that side. You want to enlarge this hole with the rotary file so that the threaded stud is dead center (Fig. 10). Thread the female end on with a screwdriver and your problem should be solved (Fig. 11).

Note that when you turn the male end with a screwdriver, the upper receiver will move back and forth. This didn't happen on the Colt lowers because the hole was in a direct line with the rear of the rifle. Chances are you won't have corrected your mistake to Colt specs, so you will have some play if you turn the screw. Adjust it for proper fit and you are good to go. Also note that every time you open the rifle, the screw will turn slightly and affect the fit. Keep a small screwdriver in your rifle case or stowaway grip for this, or carefully use the rim of a cartridge.

You must judge your own mechanical abilities before undertaking the methods to correct mistakes described above. The ideal scenario is not to make a mistake in the first place, and if you are careful you shouldn't. If you do, don't worry; it happens to the best of us!

You are now ready to begin the actual process of working your rough casting into a finished lower. Following these steps will result in the creation of a firearm that you can be proud to show off and shoot. It's not that difficult, so stick with me and I will guide you through the process.

ENLARGING THE MAGAZINE WELL

The first step I take in finishing my castings is to file the magazine well to fit. A fair amount of material needs to be removed, and I find it gives the novice a chance to get the feel for the file in a place where it doesn't really show.

It helps to determine which lower goes with which upper if you are using different caliber magazines. The placement of your upper is relevant to the front of the magazine well. The front portions of the two uppers need to match, so as you begin removing material from the heel of your top plane, it is wise to already have the magazine well sized for proper location of the upper. Keep in mind, though, that if you are using an OSI drilling jig, it fits securely into the magazine well and has been designed for M16 magazines. If you are custom-fitting a 9mm conversion block, it will not fit into the jig.

Begin by inserting your magazine into the well as far as it will go (which isn't far, if at all) until it fits snugly (Fig. 12). Use a metal M16 magazine for this, as a plastic one will be damaged from the undersized magazine well cutting into it. M16 magazines are also slightly larger than the plastic Thermold or Orlite mags, so if they drop out easily, you should have no trouble with any magazines fitting. You may need to force it a little to get it about ⅝ to ¾ inch inside. If it doesn't seem to want to go, don't force it too hard or you could damage your magazine. You may need to take what you can get and work from there.

Assuming that the magazine will in fact insert far enough to stick, turn the lower over and inspect the contact points of the magazine to the well by looking down the well from the top. Holding it up to a bright light source will easily reveal where the magazine is contacting the well (Fig. 13).

Remove the magazine and inspect the lower portion of the well. You will notice black lines on the aluminum where the magazine fit too tightly. This is where you will need to begin removing material. You might need to remove some material from the center of the well sides, but the areas of contact usually are the corners and the front. The corners generally taper slightly and merely need to be squared out, although a small amount of material might need to be removed.

Go slowly; these are cast slightly undersize for a reason—they are meant to custom-fit your magazines to the lower. If you intend to use a 120-round drum magazine, you may need to file or sand the bottom plane of the magazine well with a sanding block (Fig. 14). The shoulder of the drum may touch the bottom plane of the cast lower, keeping it from locking into the magazine catch unless some material is removed from the bottom of the well.

If you are using an Olympic Arms 9mm upper (the one that calls for Sten magazines), a conversion block is available from SOCOM Mfg. to allow you to use cheap, unmodified Sten magazines in your lower (Fig. 15). (Note: The Sten mags will only work with Oly Arms uppers. All others require expensive Colt mags.) In this application, you want the block to fit tightly in the rear portion of the well but allow your magazines to fall freely from the front portion. If you are building an AR-15 that will use M16 magazines (the norm), then you want to remove a little more material from the well to allow the magazines to drop freely upon release.

Begin by placing the casting on a hard, level surface like a workbench or coffee table (don't use the coffee table unless you are single, or want to become so again) and squaring up the corners with either a triangular file or a thin, flat file that won't make gouges with its side. (Figs. 16 and 17). A wider file is good if you need to remove material from the center of the long sides, but avoid using it in the corners because it can twist and mar the walls of the well.

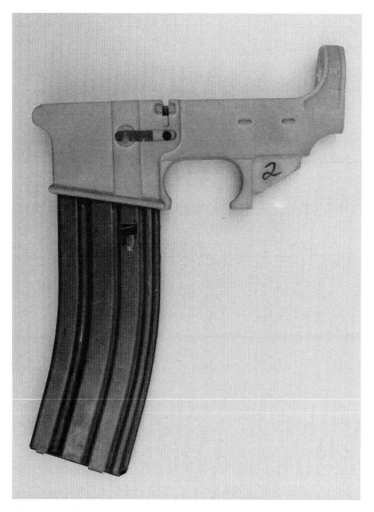

Figure 12. The magazine fits just enough to show where the tight spots are located.

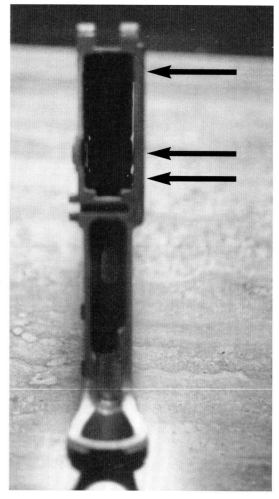

Figure 13. It was only possible to show one side of the magazine, but note the three locations where the magazine is contacting the well.

Figure 14. Sanding the magazine well.

Figure 15. If you are dedicating a particular lower to 9mm, pin or epoxy the conversion block in place to avoid dropping the entire unit by accidentally pressing the AR-15 mag release.

When working with a file, don't use a sawing motion. There are two reasons for this: it will dull the file more quickly, and you will have a tendency to remove material in the front and back but leave it high in the middle. Use firm but careful strokes, applying pressure while pushing the file away from you, then lifting it slightly on the return stroke. Once you get the hang of it, you will not only prolong the life of your file but you will get a nice, flat, uniform surface.

Check the fit of the magazine frequently to avoid removing too much material from the well. Once the magazine easily fits far enough for the square hole in it to line up with the hole for the magazine catch, you have removed enough. Hold the lower so that the magazine is vertical and let go of the mag. If it falls freely, you are finished with this step. Try this over something soft like a shop towel or a piece of carpet so you don't damage the magazine if you fail to catch it when it drops.

FITTING THE PIVOT (FRONT) LUG INTO THE CASTING

Now that you have your magazine well enlarged to accept your magazines, it's time to start fitting the upper to your lower. On the front of the casting, you will notice two "ears" that protrude frontward toward the barrel end of the lower. These ears are where the pivot pin will go, and you will most likely need to do a small amount of filing to the two inside surfaces (Fig. 18) to allow the

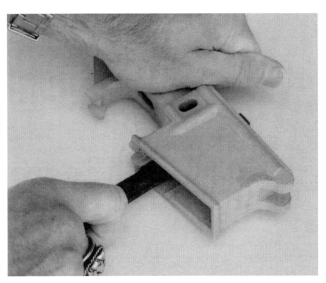

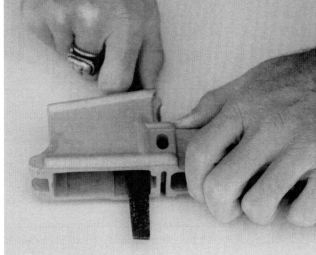

Figures 16 and 17. Squaring the corners of the magazine well with a triangular or small, flat file.

front pivot lug to fit between them. Use a fairly fine-toothed triangular file for this process—you don't want to take too much out of this space or you will have play in the lug and lower. This is one of two areas where you want as little play as possible (the other being the takedown lug). Using a triangular file also tends to alleviate any twist you might get with a wider file, which might affect the fit as well.

MILLING THE CASTING TO ACCEPT THE TAKEDOWN (REAR) LUG

The next step is to open the area where the takedown lug of your upper fits into the lower. This is the rear portion of the fire-control pocket; the area with the "shelf" in it (Fig. 19). The simplest way to fit the lug would be to file its corners off, but since the lug is still usually a little wider than the casting, you would also need to file the sides of the lug, thereby ruining the upper for use on a commercial lower should you ever decide to switch because of excessive play. Therefore, the best way is the factory way, which is to slightly mill the sides of this portion of the casting.

Depending on what you have available in your workshop, you can use a milling machine to widen the area, an XY feeding table or multidirectional vise on your drill press, or a rotary file in the press. A vertical or "overhead" milling machine is, of course, the first choice, but because they are expensive, I am going to assume you do not have one at your disposal. A multidirectional vise has a tendency to wander, so you may very easily wind up overmilling the area or at least buggering it up. This is not good. It also looks sloppy. I have used a multidirectional vise for this purpose (Fig. 20), with mixed results.

Although it takes a little longer, I prefer the rotary file because I can control the amount of material I am removing much better. A rotary file is basically a piece of hardened drill stock with vertical cutting edges that can be purchased at almost any hardware store or home center. It works like a cross between a mill and a file. I use one with a diameter of $\frac{1}{4}$ inch because it allows me to work all the way into the corners at the rear of the piece.

Hold the lower firmly with both hands and place it against the spinning rotary file (Fig. 21). Work the piece back and forth over the area from which you wish to remove material. Do this on

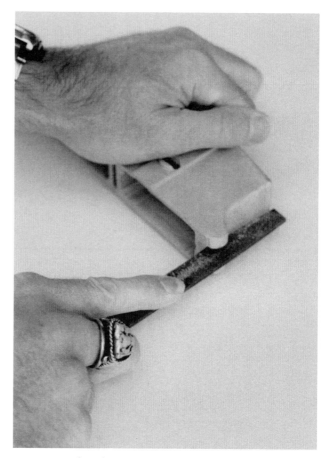

Figure 18. Filing the pivot area to accommodate the front lug.

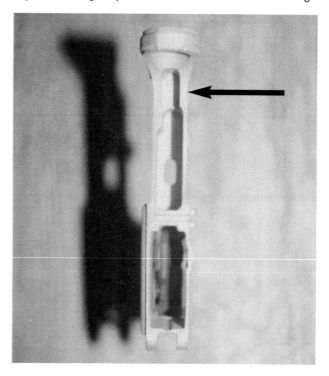

Figure 19. The "shelf" area of the casting that needs to be enlarged slightly to accept the takedown lug of the upper receiver.

Figure 20. Milling the casting for the takedown lug with a milling (multidirectional) vise.

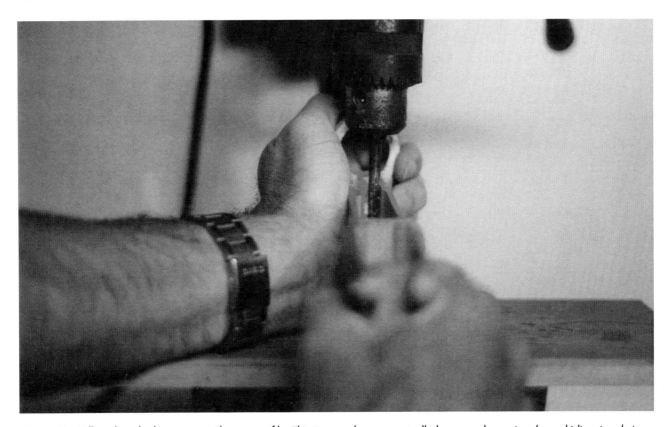

Figure 21. Milling the takedown area with a rotary file. This is a much more controlled process than using the multidirectional vise.

both sides, switching regularly so you do not remove more material from one side than the other. A fair amount of pressure works well, although if you push too hard you might create divots or move the drill press if it's a lightweight tabletop model. Check the fit of the takedown lug periodically to ensure a snug fit—you do not want a lot of play in this area!

Be careful not to elongate the center of the pocket, as a crucial vertical hole needs to be drilled just behind it in another step. If you accidentally take too much out, it will pose a problem with placement of your buffer retainer. This is more of a problem when using a milling machine or multidirectional vise; if you are using a rotary file, you most likely won't have to worry about it. Simply square the corners up with a small square file to allow the lug to fit farther back if necessary (Fig. 22).

FITTING THE TOP PLANE

Now insert the T-handle and bolt carrier into the upper and place the upper onto the lower. The back of the bolt carrier should slide into the undersized buffer tube hole, although it will most likely be off center toward the top (Fig. 23).

As you hold the lower receiver level, the bolt carrier should drop slightly anyway. You want to remove enough material from the top plane so the bolt carrier will be able to slide easily into the buffer tube once the hole is enlarged and tapped. The thickness from top to bottom of the lower casting at the trigger guard should be between 1 $\frac{5}{16}$ inch minimum and 1 $\frac{3}{8}$ inch maximum. You will experience binding in the buffer tube if the thickness is greater than 1 $\frac{3}{8}$ inch, and binding against the top of the hammer by the bolt carrier if it is less than 1 $\frac{5}{16}$ inch. The latter is less of a problem if you are measuring the placement of your holes; you will be okay if the proper distance from the top of the plane is maintained, but all measurements must then be taken from the top plane. If using a jig, then the plane will have to match the top of the jig, as all holes will be drilled to jig specs (Fig. 24).

You can use a variety of methods to mill the plane down. A floor-mounted belt sander works extremely well (Fig. 25)—too well in some cases. Be sure not to remove too much material or take more off one side than the other! I prefer files, as I can control the amount of material I am

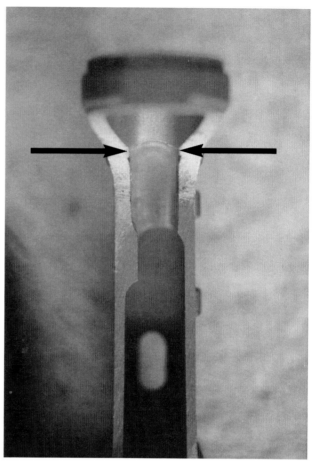

Figure 22. Here we see that the rear corners have been squared with a file to allow extra room for the lug.

Figure 23. The undersized buffer tube hole is usually cast a little low. Be sure it is centered as you enlarge it.

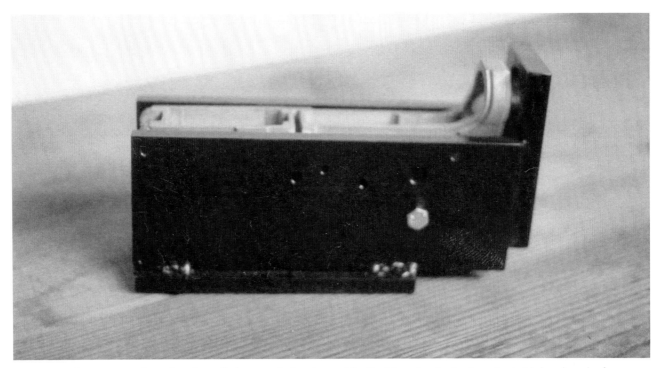

Figure 24. This casting still needs to be milled to match the plane of the jig. Note that the heel portion is higher than the front.

Figure 25. Use care when working with a belt sander! It is very easy to remove too much material.

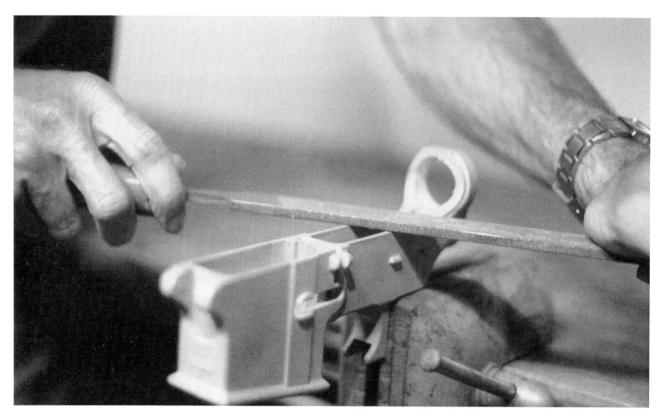

Figure 26. You can control a file much better.

removing much better (Fig. 26). The belt sander helps considerably when I run into a plane that needs quite a bit of material removed, although I would never attempt to remove all of it with the sander alone.

When removing material from the top plane or in other steps further along, it may become necessary to clamp your work in a vise. *Never* clamp the sides of the lower! You will squeeze the soft metal inward, causing a lot of extra work to open the space again. Instead, clamp the edge of the vise on the triangular web where the pistol grip attaches (Fig. 27). You can tighten the vise as much as needed on this portion of the lower without fear of damaging the casting. Should you decide you don't have enough hands to assemble everything or you want to touch something up with a file, Brownells offers a hard plastic block that locks into the magazine well via the catch for working on a lower once it's finished.

Once the depth of the plane is satisfactory, attention must be turned to the heel (curve) of the plane. This is also critical, as correct placement of the upper is crucial to proper function of the weapon. Remove material from the heel with a 1

inch diameter sanding drum on the drill press (Fig. 28) or the convex side of a half-round file (Fig. 29). A rattail file can be used as a last resort, but care must be taken not to create grooves. Some 60 grit sandpaper wrapped around a piece of broomstick will help to dress out any grooves you might make with a rattail file.

The way to check the fit of the upper into the heel of the lower is to insert your finger into the magazine well and feel for the front portion of the well in the upper. When the fit feels smooth (no step), they are aligned properly. Hopefully you took your time when removing material from the heel and have a nice, tight fit. At this point it may be necessary to remove a little more material from the rear corners of the takedown pocket (the rear portion of the fire-control pocket where the takedown lug fits into the lower receiver) to get the lug to move far enough back to allow the upper to seat properly.

ENLARGING THE BUFFER TUBE HOLE

The best way to enlarge the buffer tube hole enough to tap it for the threaded buffer tube is to

Figure 27. Always clamp your lower in this manner. To access the other end of the casting, simply turn it and place it in the opposite end of the vise.

Figure 28. Remove most of the metal with the 1 inch drum sander if you have one. Your files and sanding tools can become clogged if you are working with aluminum; try spraying a little Pam on them to help prevent this.

Figure 29. Use a half-round file for the finishing touches or for the whole process if you don't have a set of sanding drums. This file is flat on one side but rounded on the other.

use a 1⅛ inch drill bit and/or reamer that can be bought from most suppliers of jigs and castings. They are expensive, but with a little ingenuity, you need not spend the money if you are only making one rifle.

For my first three rifles I used a drum sander with a piece of ½ grit floor-sanding paper wrapped and duct-taped to it. This went in the chuck of an electric drill and acted like a rotary rasp. As the hole enlarged I shimmed the sandpaper out with strips of paper, creating a slight cone shape to the drum and paper that allowed me to enlarge the hole as I moved the drum further in. This method is rather time-consuming, but it will save you some money if you don't wish to spend any more than you absolutely need. (I present both professional and improvisational methods in this book so that everyone can accomplish this rewarding task, even without a metal shop.)

I have since purchased a 1⅛ inch drill bit along with a drilling jig, and the time and effort it saved me was well worth the money! You *must* use a variable-speed drill with this large bit or the chatter will give you a square hole. A good battery-powered drill works great (Fig. 30). Just barely turn the bit and you will be able to control your progress easily. Just make sure your casting is clamped securely by the web, and check often to be sure you are drilling straight.

If you use a reamer the hole will be the exact size you need, but if you go with an alternative method, keep in mind that the hole needs to be big enough so that the tap will only thread the hole and not shave it with the front end. I almost ruined one lower by doing just that. The buffer tube in that particular lower is really only being held by three threads, but if it ever comes loose, some cold weld and rethreading will solve that. Remember, you are benefiting from all the mistakes I've already made. Using the proper tools and a jig will alleviate most of them. Improvisers, pay attention.

THREADING THE BUFFER TUBE HOLE

If you've spent the money for an OSI Super Jig, it will have the buffer tube hole guide threaded. All you have to do is thread the tap into

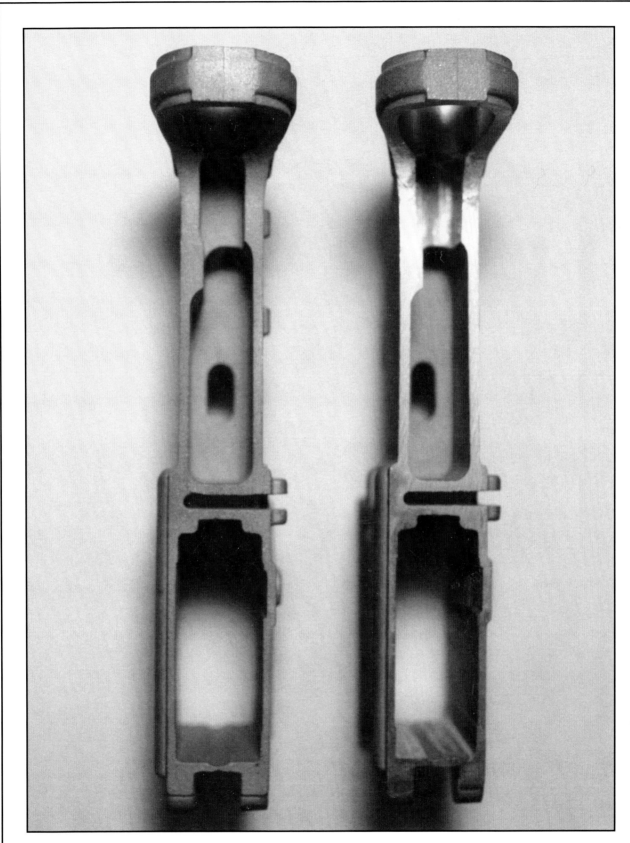

Here we see a raw casting (left) and a casting finished thus far. Note the shiny surfaces on the top plane and in the buffer tube hole.

Figure 30. Drilling the buffer tube hole.

the hole and continue until the threads are cut into the receiver (Fig. 31). If you are using the alternative method, clamp the lower vertically into a vise by the pistol grip web. Apply a little bit of oil to the end of the tap, and go slowly; make about a quarter turn at a time. Turn the tap back slightly each time to keep the threads cleaned out and to prevent stripping them.

If you do not have a tap handle large enough to accommodate the ½ inch end of the 1³⁄₁₆ x 16 TPI starting tap (most of us don't), a ¹⁵⁄₁₆ inch or 23mm socket will slide over it. With a ratcheting handle, you now have the ability to tap the hole (Fig. 32). Take your time! If you are not careful, you can easily tap the threads crooked and cause yourself a terrible headache. Fortunately the thread is coarse, which allows you to straighten it out if need be without stripping the threads. This is accomplished by applying pressure to the side that is leaning toward the center of the hole.

Once you think you have it going straight, remove the tap and thread the tube into the hole. This is the best way to check whether or not your threads are still straight. They need to be straight

both vertically and horizontally or else the bolt carrier will not fit all the way into the buffer tube, or it will hang up partway.

ENLARGING THE FIRE-CONTROL POCKET

The next step in readying the casting is milling the edges of the fire-control pocket. On a lot of castings, the sides will shrink inward slightly during cooling, giving a slightly concave surface. Sometimes it is negligible; other times it is distinctly noticeable. Before milling the side walls, it is best to straighten the sides as much as possible if they are noticeably concave. This will not only save you time and work but will also keep as much material on the sides of the receiver as possible.

Start by securely clamping the lower in your vise at the web. Insert the handle from a ½ inch drive ratchet into the pocket and *gently* but firmly pry it against each side of the lower. This will open the sides and straighten everything up. Once the sides are nice and straight, try slipping the hammer into the pocket. At this point it should still

Figure 31. Thread the tap into the OSI jig and continue into the hole of the casting.

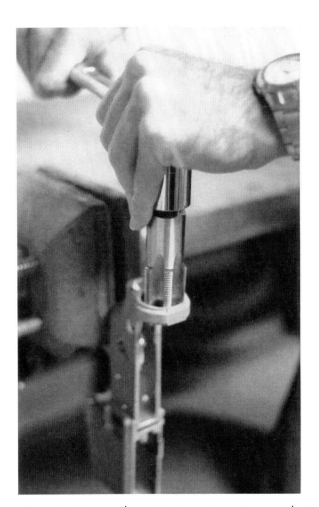

Figure 32. Tapping the casting in a vise, using a ratcheting socket to turn the large tap.

be too tight for the hammer or trigger to fit, so head for the milling machine or rotary file and begin removing material from the sides in the same manner as shown in Figure 21.

You may find that some areas need more work than others; the hammer might fit first, then you might need to work on the trigger area. Each lower is unique in its casting, so just expect to custom-mill everything. Some people will simply grind the hubs of the hammer and trigger down, but that will ruin them for use in other lowers as well as prevent you from switching parts in your own lower later on (if, for example, you wish to install a match trigger).

Once your hammer and trigger can slide into place on the receiver, touching up the area with a smooth file will assure smooth action of the parts as well as make everything look more professional. Just be careful not to remove any more material than is necessary; you do not want the hammer to wander during firing and wear against the sides of the receiver.

You are now ready to begin drilling your holes.

DRILLING YOUR HOLES WITHOUT THE AID OF A JIG

Pivot and Takedown Pin Holes

You are now ready to begin drilling the holes

Figure 33. Laying an upper on the lower receiver to mark the holes.

in your casting. We will start with the pivot and takedown pin holes. If you are doing this without the aid of a jig, start by laying the upper receiver onto the top plane of the lower with the lugs positioned on the *outside* of your casting (Fig. 33). Make sure the upper is tight to the heel of the lower. (You may need to push the forward assist inward slightly to clear the buffer tube hole when laying the upper on the "selector lever" side.) Once the two pieces are tight together, trace the inside of the lug holes onto the outside of your casting with a scratch awl, or use a centering bore (more on this below). You may wish to shim the two receivers apart slightly with a piece of paper to reduce your tolerances, but that is a personal decision. If you feel you can hit the nail on the head, so to speak, you may not care to shim them.

One thing to mention before I go any further is that the takedown pin will actually recess slightly into the magazine-release button (hereafter designated MRB) side of the casting. You will need to slightly enlarge and countersink the hole on this side with a ⅜ inch pilot point, or "bullet bit." It basically works like a Forstner bit does on wood; it has a centering point and "cleans out" the material,

leaving a flat bottom to the hole as opposed to the normally pointed bottom. I strongly recommend making this countersink *first*, then drilling the smaller hole in the center divot. Make a divot with the regular bit, then use the bullet bit to make your recessed hole.

You can try to enlarge the hole after you drill it with a standard ⅜ inch bit, but I wouldn't recommend it for two reasons. First, the chatter will bugger up the hole, and second, even if you do somehow manage to get the hole round, the bottom will not be flat. The conical hole will interfere with the takedown detent and cause a lot of problems (trust me; I've made this mistake). Spend the few extra dollars to purchase the proper tool for the job and obtain a professional-looking result. It can be found as part of a set in the tool corral of your local home center or individually at a commercial tool company.

Repeat the marking process on the opposite side. If you have a variable-speed drill, you can use the ¼ inch drill bit for the pivot and takedown pin holes to actually drill through at this point instead of merely marking the receiver and drilling them out on the drill press. I, however, would advise

Figure 34. Drilling the pivot pin hole.

against it because you might remove additional material from the lugs as well. This is your call; I am merely demonstrating the various methods of drilling these holes without the use of a jig. You can also spin the drill just enough to make a small indentation, then drill the hole out on the drill press (although the centering bore is superior for this).

If you have elected to drill through the casting using the lugs as a guide, you are finished with this step. If not, continue reading and I will explain how to drill them with the drill press.

If you have made the indentation with the drill bit in the previous step, you are ready to use it as a drilling locator. If not, carefully place the scratch awl or center punch in the center of the scratched circle, then tap a few times with a hammer to make an indentation in which to place the drill bit for drilling.

To actually begin drilling on your press, you must take care to ensure that your casting is perfectly level. Otherwise you will drill your holes on an angle, which will ruin this part of the process.

To drill the pivot hole on the magazine catch (hereafter MC) side of the casting, simply place the

casting on a flat piece of wood that is small enough to allow the buffer tube portion of the casting to overhang. The reinforcement areas of the magazine well are the same thickness, so it will lay level. While holding the two pieces firmly, slowly bring the bit onto your work (Fig. 34). Make sure it is lined up on the divot, and slowly but evenly drill through *one side only*. This is in case your work is not perfectly level. The hole will not be drilled into the wrong location on the other side of the casting.

To drill the hole on the MRB side, you will need to shim the casting off of your drilling board. On the MC side, you will note the raised portions on the casting (the mag well lip and the raised area where the magazine catch is). Slide your shim between these portions and turn the whole thing over. This will allow you to keep your work level while drilling the pivot hole on the MRB side. Repeat the drilling process, again making sure to hold the work firmly while you drill carefully.

There will be a slight burr on the inside of the "takedown ears" due to drilling that will need to be removed with a smooth file. File just enough to remove the burrs but not any excess material. Slip your pivot pin through the holes. If they don't line

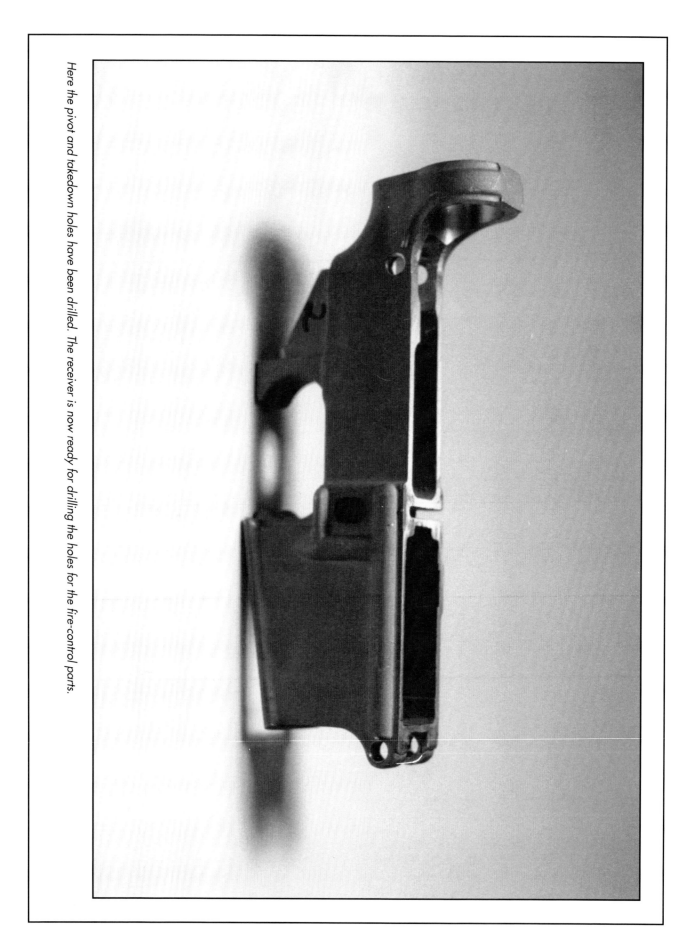

Here the pivot and takedown holes have been drilled. The receiver is now ready for drilling the holes for the fire-control parts.

up completely (they will most likely be a hair off), you can make a quick pass with the drill bit in the hand drill. If they are off significantly, put the pivot lug in the ears and see which hole is off. It may become necessary to slightly elongate one hole or the other with the ¼ inch rotary file. Work carefully, and don't rush. Keep trying the fit of the pin. If your tolerances are tight but the pin just won't go all the way through, it may become necessary to make a quick pass with the drill again. Once the holes are aligned, insert the pivot pin through the hole and see how the upper fits into the lower. If it looks good, then you are ready to drill the rear takedown holes.

To drill the takedown hole on the MC side of the casting, place a small block of wood under the fire-control area of the casting on the MRB side (i.e., the smooth portion behind the magazine catch hole) and drill your ¼ inch hole in the same manner as the pivot pin.

You will need a shim for the last hole in this step. Place the same small block of wood against the two selector "horns" on the MC side of the casting and turn the whole thing over. Drill your last hole in the same manner as the other three, then insert your pivot pin to hold both receivers.

Close the upper into the lower and try inserting the takedown pin from the MRB side. It should fit. This is usually a very tight fit because not only do you have your holes lined up, you lined them up with the upper tight to the lower. If you placed the paper shim between the lowers when marking your holes, the fit should be easier because of the little area of play it created. A tight fit will usually loosen up after you have fired a number of rounds through the rifle.

Personally, I don't mind a really tight fit on the takedown pin because I never installed pivot or takedown detents on any of my rifles. This isn't as big a deal with the pivot pin, because early Colts didn't have them either. You can still purchase the old-style pivot pin; it's a little longer and has a ball detent built into it to keep it from falling out.

If you don't want to attempt drilling the pivot or takedown detent holes, you might choose these old-style pins for both roles. The pivot pin is longer than the takedown pin, however, so if you use the pivot pin for a takedown pin, it will stick out on the sides. If you don't mind the pin protruding, you have just eliminated two more steps from your project.

The better method to avoid drilling a takedown detent hole is to use a rear tensioning pin. Available from Brownells, this pin expands as you turn it to lock firmly in place. I recommend this pin for the takedown if you do not want to drill the detent hole.

Hammer, Trigger, and Selector Holes

These are undoubtedly the six most important holes you will drill in your casting and the most critical in terms of tolerance. The rifle will actually fire without any other holes being drilled; these are the ones you cannot do without, and they must be accurate!

Now that your pivot and takedown holes are drilled, you can use an existing AR-15 lower for a *marking* jig. Do not attempt to use the lower as a *drilling* jig or you will hog out the holes in it and ruin it.

Start by inserting ¼ inch drill bits through the takedown and pivot holes in both receivers to lock them together (Fig. 35). This will align the receivers so you can mark where the holes will be drilled in your casting. You can use the scratch awl to mark these holes, but a centering bore is the better choice. A centering bore is basically a piece of drill rod with a sharp point but no cutting edges that will ruin the piece you are using for a guide. It is designed specifically for this purpose and can be obtained at a tool supply house. It will cut a small divot dead center and alleviate the task of trying to find the exact center of your mark with an awl or center punch. You then lower your #24 (.152) bit on the drill press into the divot and drill your hole exactly where you want it. You need to shim the lower for drilling these holes, but you have already done this once before when drilling your takedown holes.

Once you have drilled your holes, check to see if they are aligned in both directions by putting the drill bit through each hole and inspecting it to see if the bit looks straight. If it does, you are ready to install your hammer and trigger to test them. If you have purchased a lower parts kit, you will need to put the spring on your hammer (Fig. 36) and trigger (Fig. 37). You do not need to put the disconnector on the trigger at this point because this is only a test; you will be removing these parts to continue the drilling process.

Install the trigger first by positioning it and pushing your pin through (Fig. 38). You may need to tap the pin carefully with a hammer the first

Figure 35. Two z\v inch drill bits will lock the receivers together so that you can mark your holes.

time or so because the hole will be tight. Avoid inserting and removing these pins any more than you have to, as the more times you do it, the more you will loosen the fit.

Repeat this process with the hammer (Fig. 39). Take your time; it can be tricky to line everything up just right. The tolerances between the pin and hammer are very tight. Again, don't worry about adding the disconnector at this point.

Once the trigger and hammer are in place, carefully cock the hammer back. If it clicks into place easily, you are halfway there. Holding the heel of your hand against the hammer face (dry-firing at this point will damage the front of the fire-control pocket), gently pull the trigger. If it releases, then you are well on your way to having a working rifle.

Inspect the hammer in its upright position. See if it looks straight. If it does, cock it again and inspect it in the reclining position. Still straight? Good. If not, measure your holes against those in the lower you used as a marking jig and see which one is off. You will then need to fill the hole with cold weld or aluminum solder and re-drill.

Drill the selector hole with a ³⁄₈ inch bit, shimming the receiver in the same manner as you did for the hammer and trigger pin holes (Fig. 40). Check the fit of the selector, then remove it.

Assuming that everything is copacetic at this

Figure 36. Hammer and spring. This is the way most springs come in a parts kit, but the short portion actually goes on the back of the hammer, not the front. Simply turn it until the short portion touches the back. Do not install it with the short side to the rear or it will be backwards!

Figure 37. Trigger and spring.

Figure 38. Trigger installed in the casting.

Figure 39. With the hammer installed, it is possible to cock and dry-fire the lower. Catch the hammer with your hand; do not let it strike the front of the fire-control pocket.

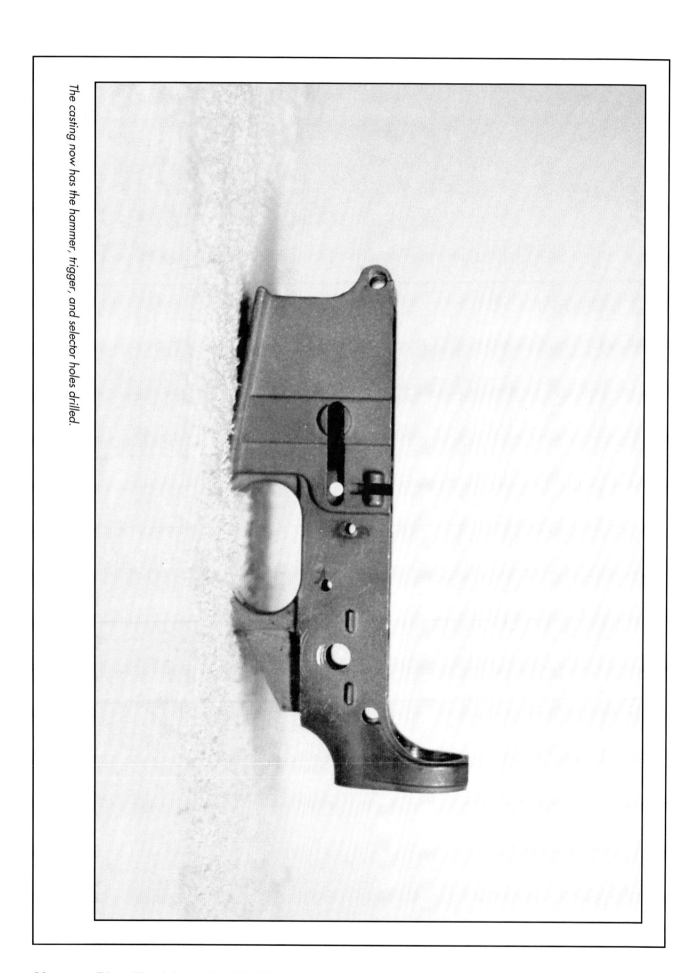

The casting now has the hammer, trigger, and selector holes drilled.

Figure 40. Use a wooden block to shim the receiver and drill your selector hole.

point, put your upper receiver onto your lower and pin it in place. Cycle the action by hand. There is no buffer tube assembly or spring to return it for you, so you will have to push the bolt carrier forward until it locks in place. Now you can dry-fire the action. If it releases and hits the firing pin (which it should), the hardest part is over. You are now ready to drill the buffer retainer hole.

Buffer Retainer (Detent) Hole

This hole can be a little tricky, as it needs to be drilled on a slight angle. If you attempt to drill it straight down past the buffer ring, it will end up halfway into the fire-control pocket. Therefore, you must shim underneath the rear of the magazine well (Fig. 41) to angle it enough. The thickness of a typical yardstick (about $3/16$ inch) is ideal. You want this hole as close to the center of the casting as possible, although it isn't that critical. This is one of the few holes that can be slightly off one way or the other without causing a major problem. The thing to remember is that the buffer tube must protrude over the shoulder of the

Figure 41. Drilling the buffer retainer hole. A yardstick is the perfect thickness for a shim.

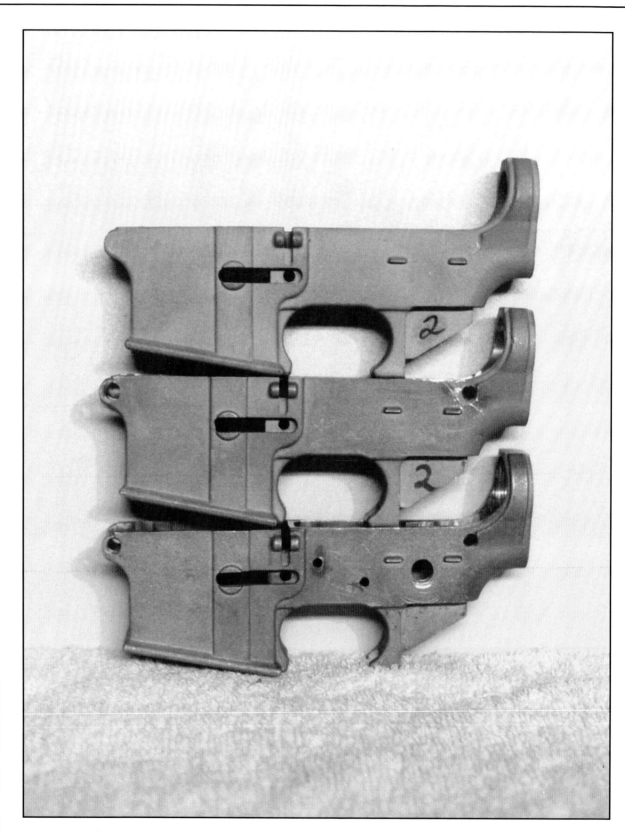

Comparison of the steps completed so far. The receiver on top is a raw casting. The one in the middle is milled out and has the pivot and takedown holes drilled. The one on the bottom has the buffer tube hole drilled and tapped and the holes for the fire-control parts drilled.

detent to hold it in place yet not touch the raised tip, which holds the buffer in place. It is an ingenious design.

When drilling this hole, take great care not to bore too deeply or you will drill through the underside of the casting! You will need a ¼ inch drill for this. Take your time, and check the depth frequently. You want it just deep enough— approximately ¹¹⁄₁₆ inch—to be able to seat the detent so its tip is flush with the surface of the buffer hole. Make sure you have the spring situated under the detent when you push it into the hole; otherwise it will get stuck and you will find it nearly impossible to remove.

Pistol Grip Screw Hole

This hole is fairly easy to locate and drill. Slip your grip on the web of the casting and trace the hole in the grip onto the casting with a pencil. Remove the grip, locate the center of the hole, and mark it with a center punch or awl. This hole needs to be bored perpendicular to the surface of the web, so you will need to either hold it firmly or shim it (Fig. 42) when drilling. Bore this hole all

the way into the fire-control pocket with a #7 (.201) bit, and clean the hole with a few more passes of the bit. You are now ready to tap this hole with a ¼ x 28 TPI tap.

This is the one time you will not be able to clamp your casting by the pistol grip web. Carefully place it in your vise as shown in Figure 43 and tighten just enough to hold it snugly. Do not overtighten! Place a few drops of oil on the end of your tap and thread the hole all the way into the fire-control pocket.

DRILLING YOUR HOLES USING AN OSI JIG

The OSI drilling jig will make your job a whole lot easier if you wish to finish a few castings into rifles. The casting fits into the jig via the magazine well, so you will still need to enlarge it first. Once your top plane is milled to match the plane of the jig, you merely need to use the aforementioned bits in their respective holes. A word of caution, however: drill your buffer tube hole *before* you put the casting in the jig. If you attempt to drill it in

Figure 42. Drilling the pistol grip screw hole.

Figure 43. Tapping the pistol grip screw hole.

Figure 44. Using a hand drill to make the pivot hole.

Figure 45. Using a drill press to drill the takedown hole in one pass.

place, you will ruin the threads on the jig. Lock the casting into place with the two set screws and you are ready to begin drilling.

The jig is designed to help you drill the fire-control (hammer, trigger, and selector) holes with a drill press. All other holes should be drilled with a variable-speed hand drill.

Pivot and Takedown Holes

Drill the pivot and takedown holes first—the jig comes with a set of pins that will fit through these holes to lock the casting into position for drilling the hammer, trigger, and selector holes. Drill the pivot and takedown holes from each side with a hand drill (Fig. 44) or in the drill press (Fig. 45) using the jig as a guide. This will ensure that they line up, and there is less tendency to drill on an angle. Drill slowly and carefully, as the jig is not hardened and can be damaged if you twist the drill or use too high a speed.

Once all four holes have been drilled (two from each side), insert the pins through the holes in the jig to hold the casting securely. You are now ready to drill the critical fire-control holes.

Hammer, Trigger, and Selector Holes

These holes should all be drilled with the drill press (as in Figure 45). The hand drill will allow too much wobble, and your holes will not line up (Fig. 46). There is no particular order to drilling these holes, but perform the same assembly/testing steps as described above to ensure they have been drilled correctly.

Pistol Grip Screw Hole

Aside from the butt stock lug hole, this is the last hole that can be drilled with the jig. Since this hole is on a 45 degree angle, you will need to use the hand drill. Drill all the way into the fire-control pocket.

Butt Stock Lug Hole

This is actually the last mandatory hole in order to produce a working rifle. It serves only to lock the butt stock into place and keep it from twisting. There is a hole in the OSI jig for the lug, so it is a simple hole to drill. After this step, you may put the jig away. It has served its honorable purpose.

If you are using the improvisational method, screw the buffer tube into the receiver and slip the butt stock onto it. Align the stock to where you want it and scribe around the lug with an awl. Remove

Figure 46. Do not use the hand drill for this portion of the project!

the stock and tube and center the rough circle you have just made. Make your divot and carefully drill a ½ inch hole ⅛ inch deep. That should be far enough. Double-check by sliding the stock back on. It is not a problem if it needs a little more material removed, because you can actually drill all the way into the fire-control pocket and not affect the function of the rifle. This is not done on a factory lower, so there is no need to drill that far on yours.

THE REMAINING STEPS DO NOT REQUIRE THE JIG AND MUST BE DONE BY HAND

Selector Detent Hole

This hole must align exactly with the center of the selector hole. Using your existing lower as a reference, mark dead center between the web and outside of the casting (Fig. 47) and dead center over the selector hole (Fig. 48). This is a "stepped hole," so it must be drilled first with a #31 (.120) bit, then partway with a #27 (.144) bit. This is to keep the detent itself from falling into the selector hole if you remove the selector. It is fairly cut-and-dry to drill; with the casting turned upside down, simply place a block of wood under the top plane to hold it level and drill your first hole all the way through. If it is dead center (or fairly close) of the selector hole, it should be alright. Enlarge the hole with the #31 (.120) bit to a depth of ¼ inch.

To test your detent, you will need to insert the selector, then drop the detent in the hole, insert the detent spring into the pistol grip, and screw the grip in place. It can be very difficult to get everything lined up, and it is common to have the selector fall out in this step. Be patient; it can take awhile, even if you are used to doing it. When screwing the grip on, it is wise to use a magnetic

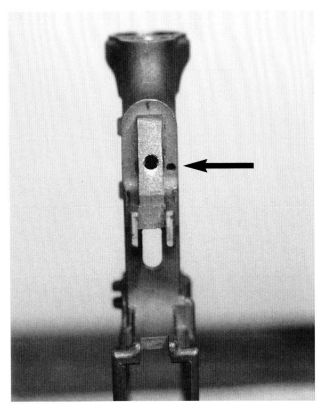

Figure 47. Location of the selector detent hole.

screwdriver if you have one, as it can be tricky to get the screw into the hole otherwise.

Once everything is together, try rotating the selector. It should turn freely without binding yet not be loose. It may take awhile to break in if your hole is off a little. A little touch of grease on the tip of the detent should help with any sticking.

I know it took you forever to get everything put in to test the selector detent, but it must all be removed to continue drilling the rest of the holes. It will be much easier the next time you do it now that you know what to expect.

Bolt Hold-Open Catch Spring and Pin (Optional)

These last three steps are not mandatory for the function of the rifle, although they are certainly convenient. They will be presented in the order of most importance, starting with the bolt hold-open catch. The catch will require the drilling of two holes: one for the pin and the other for a spring.

I like the bolt hold-open feature because it

Figure 48. Make sure you drill straight! This is how the hole should be lined up.

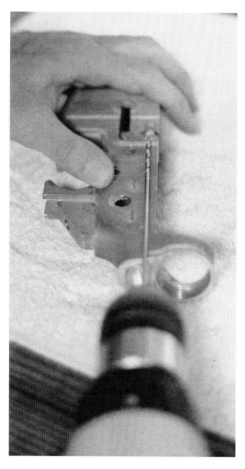

Figure 49. Drilling the hole for the bolt catch pin.

Figure 50. A six-penny common nail makes an ideal pin if your hole is slightly oversized. Keep the nail intact until final assembly, then trim to length.

allows you to insert a fresh magazine and slam the bolt shut without having to re-cock the rifle, but you may decide to skip this step. If you are building a 9mm rifle, for example, it takes a different catch anyway. There are also many assault-type weapons that don't have this feature and work very well, most notably the AK-47. For those who wish to include it on their rifle, read on.

To drill the pin hole, you will need a $\frac{3}{32}$ x 6 inch drill bit. Drill from back to front (Fig. 49). A shim will help to hold the bit level. If your hole ends up slightly oversized, the roll pin will be too loose; however, a six-penny nail with the point ground off and rounded is the perfect diameter (Fig. 50)! It is also a lot easier to remove than the roll pin and need only be trimmed to final length just before you assemble the rifle for the last time.

The hole for the spring is rather critical. Drilling it too low will put it into your magazine-catch button well; too high, and it will wander

through the edge and into the catch itself. Drill just below the edge with a #24 (.152) bit (Fig. 51), and you should be fine.

Pivot Pin and Takedown Detents (Optional)

Both of these steps can be eliminated if you really don't wish to undertake them. A ball-detent pivot pin can be used in lieu of the standard pivot pin and detent, and a tensioning takedown pin can be used in place of the standard takedown pin if you wish to avoid drilling the tricky hole for the takedown detent.

The pivot pin detent hole is fairly easy to drill, but the takedown pin detent hole is a little trickier. It is over an inch long, and the bit can easily wander during the process. For the pivot detent, rest the $\frac{5}{64}$ inch drill bit on the pivot ear (Fig. 52) and bore in about $\frac{7}{8}$ inch. To drill the takedown detent, eyeball the center of the takedown hole (or draw a line with a ruler) and make a correlating mark on the back of the receiver. Measure in exactly 2mm from the outside edge and make a mark with the center punch. You may need to use a drill press vise for this step (Fig. 53). Make sure the casting is plumb in both directions before drilling! The hole needs to be between 2mm and $\frac{1}{16}$ inch where it enters the takedown hole or else the detent will not function properly.

Trigger Guard Pins (Optional)

This is the final step prior to assembly and, quite frankly, is unneeded in my opinion. I will cover it anyway, because it is part of a factory rifle. You cannot shoot an AR-15 with gloves or trigger mittens with the guard in position, and it can be a pain to open when you need it out of the way. You need access to a firing pin or some other equally thin object to push in the detent pin to drop the guard. In addition, if you apply too much pressure when drilling the pin holes, you can very easily snap the brittle casting. Again, I recommend

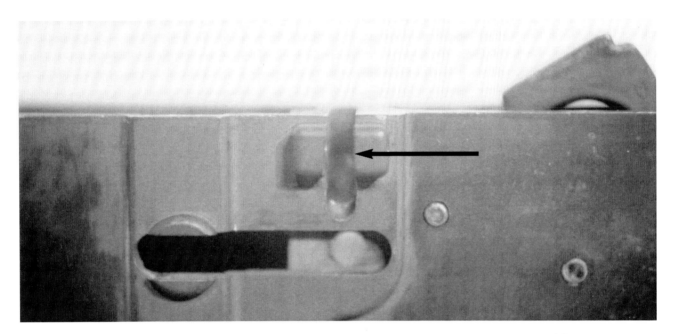

Figure 51. Location of the hole for the bolt catch spring. There is little room for error on this one, so drill carefully.

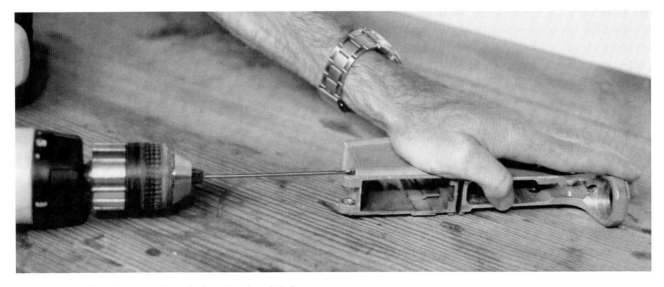

Figure 52. Drilling the pivot detent hole with a hand drill.

omitting this part from your project rifle. (Another option is to use a casting with the trigger guard cast in place. They cost a few dollars more but can be well worth the price if you want the look of the trigger guard without the hassle of drilling or risking a broken casting.)

These holes will need to be drilled by eye, even if you do have a jig, because they are not included in the jig.

Lay the trigger guard in the groove on the bottom of the lower (Fig. 54) so that the end with the roll pin hole is *behind* the trigger (i.e., near the pistol grip). The front end of the guard should be flush with the edge of the magazine well. Bring the pin hole end down until it just clears the groove (Fig. 55), and mark the center on the casting. Measure in ⅛ inch and drill with a #30 (.128) bit. Do not apply too much pressure or you can snap this part of the casting! On this one you can pass the bit all the way through if you'd like, or you can drill from each side as with all the other holes. One way will require you to file on the inside only; the other will need filing on the outside of the casting

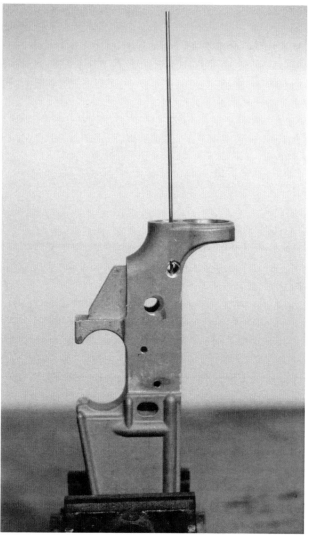

Figure 53. This is how your work should be positioned when drilling the takedown detent hole using a drill press vise. You will need a full-size drill press for this one, though, as the vise takes up too much room in a smaller press.

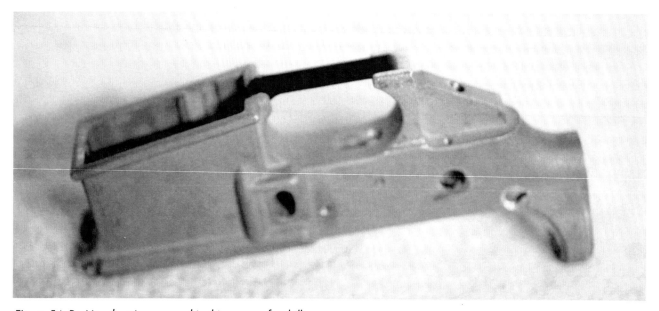

Figure 54. Position the trigger guard in this manner for drilling.

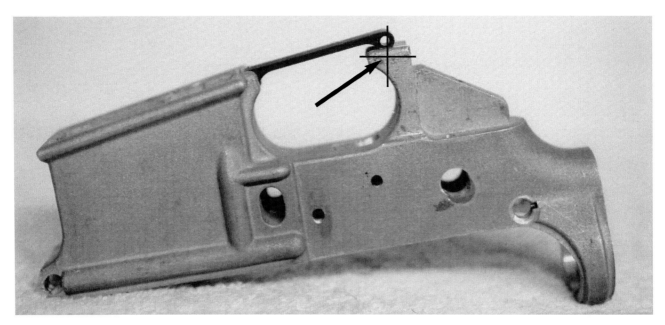

Figure 55. Marking the casting for drilling.

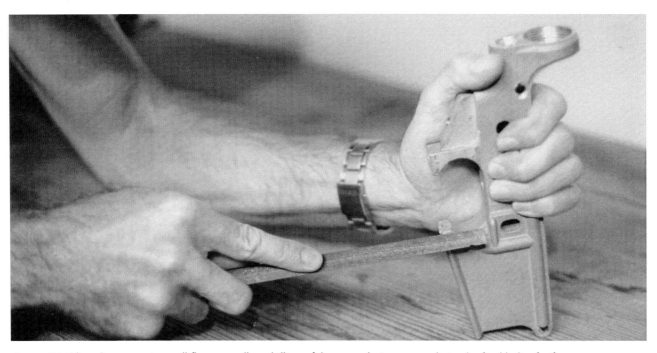

Figure 56. Filing the magazine well flange to allow drilling of the second trigger guard pin, the final hole of a factory-spec lower receiver.

as well. Your call.

Now comes the really tricky part and the reason most people don't attempt fitting the trigger guard in the first place. You will need to file a portion of the magazine well flange (Fig. 56) to have enough room to bore your final hole. This is done on the *MRB side only!* Place the #30 (.128) drill bit in the rear pin hole to hold the guard in place while you line up the final hole for drilling with a #31 (.120) bit. You will have to line up this final hole by eye and hold your breath. If it fits, you are now ready to begin assembly of your completed AR-15 casting for testing and firing.

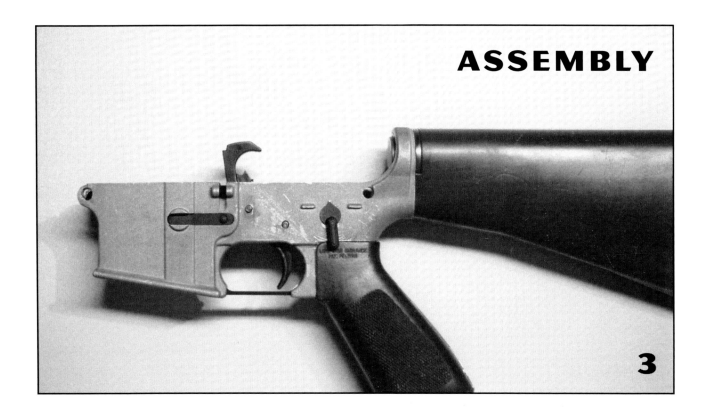

ASSEMBLY

Congratulations! You have succeeded in finishing an 80 percent AR-15 casting into a working lower. Now you just need to follow a few steps for assembling it into a working *rifle*. You may choose to finish the casting before you assemble it for testing or after. If you want to test-fire it first, leave the trigger guard, magazine catch, and pivot pin detent off for the testing process, as they will be difficult to remove to apply the finish later (almost impossible for the detent). If you are using a prefinished lower from The Tannery Shop, the problem is already solved. These are also the optional parts that you might not even have on your rifle. If you have readied the lower for these parts, however, I would test-fire the rifle first. Therefore, the chapter on finishing will come after we cover assembly and test-firing.

OVERVIEW OF ALL AR-15 LOWER PARTS

Figure 57 shows every part, pin, and spring needed for building an AR-15 lower. Some parts are very similar both in size or shape, so pay careful attention when trying to fit them. I will note the similar parts and explain their differences.

Illustrated step-by-step instruction in the assembly of the lower parts is beyond the scope of this book. You can obtain concise instructions on the Internet and in several books and manuals. The main purpose of this book is to present you with detailed instructions on how to finish a casting into a working rifle, a subject unavailable anywhere else.

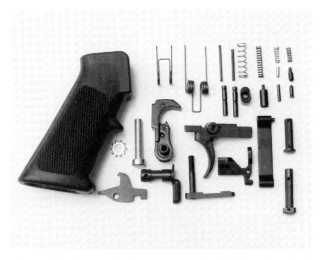

Figure 57. A complete lower parts kit, including the pistol grip, screw, and washer.

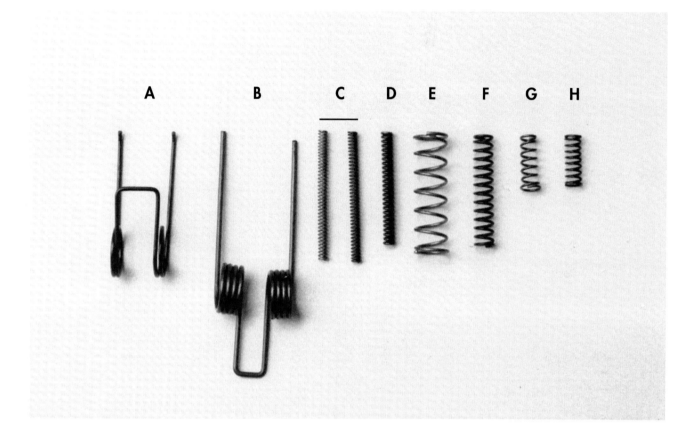

Springs

A. *Trigger spring*—The smaller of the two leverage springs.

B. *Hammer spring*—The heavier of the leverage springs. It has more coils on each side and is of heavier-gauge wire.

C. *Pivot detent/takedown detent springs*—There are two of these long, skinny springs. They are slightly longer and thinner than the selector spring.

D. *Selector spring*—Looks similar to the pivot detent/takedown detent springs, but there will only be one of these. It is a little thicker but slightly shorter.

E. *Magazine catch spring*—This is the largest coil spring in the lower parts kit.

F. *Buffer detent spring*—Second largest coil spring in the parts kit.

G. *Disconnector spring*—One end is wider than the other (tapered). It is the same length as the bolt catch spring.

H. *Bolt catch spring*—This can be readily confused with the disconnector spring, but again, the disconnector spring is tapered.

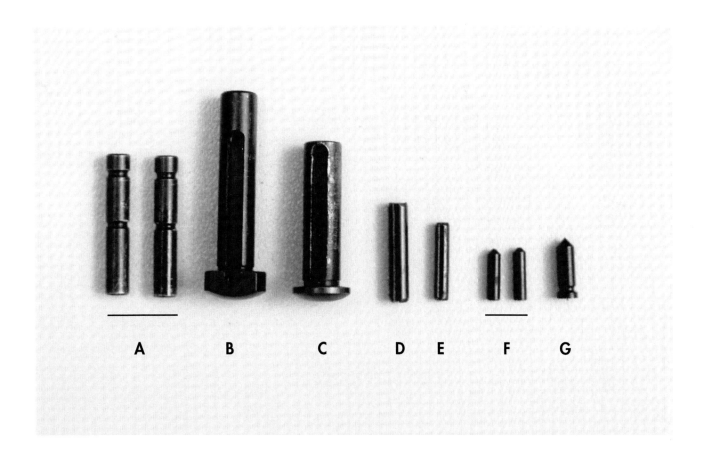

Pins and Detents

A. *Hammer/trigger pins*—There are two of these. The end with the groove in it should be used as the "head" end.

B. *Pivot pin*—The longer of the two large, grooved pins.

C. *Takedown pin*—The shorter of the two large, grooved pins.

D. *Trigger guard roll pin*—The larger of the two roll pins.

E. *Bolt catch roll pin*—The smaller of the two roll pins.

F. *Pivot/takedown detents*—There are two of these. They are the smallest detents, rounded on both ends.

G. *Selector detent*—Looks like a miniature pistol cartridge; one end is flat, the other pointed.

Large Parts

A. *Hammer*
B. *Trigger*
C. *Disconnector*
D. *Selector*
E. *Trigger guard*—May be either plastic or aluminum, depending on parts kit supplier.
F. *Magazine catch*
G. *Magazine catch button*—May be either plastic or aluminum, depending on parts kit supplier.
H. *Pistol grip screw*

Note: I left out the grip in this photo because it is obvious.

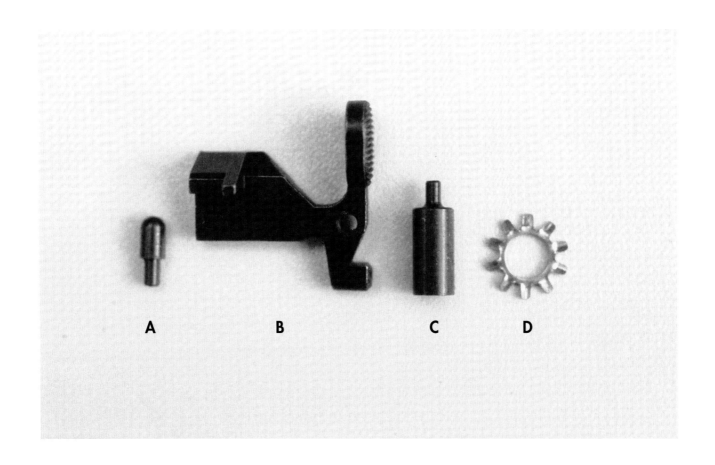

Small Parts

A. *Bolt catch buffer*
B. *Bolt catch*
C. *Buffer detent*—Hollow to accept the detent spring.
D. *Pistol grip lock washer*

ASSEMBLING THE PARTS

Now that you are familiar with all the parts, springs, pins, and detents, expect to spend about one to two hours putting everything together. The more experienced you become at this, the quicker it will go on future projects. I can do it in about 20 to 30 minutes, but this is because I have been putting these things together for many years, both as homebuilt projects and as stripped commercial lowers I have made into complete rifles. I have been interested in AR-15s since the late 1980s and have been building them for almost as long.

When you buy a parts kit, it is very likely that each part will have a light coat of Cosmoline or some other rust-inhibiting coating. Spray or soak the parts with degreaser or gun scrubber, then lightly coat them with Rem Oil or a similar quality gun oil. (*Never* use WD-40 on a firearm! It will gum up.) Take particular care not to get any oil on the face of your bolt when cleaning and oiling the entire weapon later on.

Before assembly, blow out all the recesses in your casting with compressed air to ensure that no shavings get into the parts. This will also make it easier to spot dust or shavings later on should some of the parts wear against the sides of the casting.

Figure 58. Magazine catch assembly.

Magazine Catch

Let's start with the magazine catch assembly (Fig. 58). If you have elected to skip ahead and prefinish your casting or have purchased one that has already been anodized or epoxied, you must be very careful during this step or you could scratch the finish. Begin by placing the magazine catch into the recess on the MC side of the receiver.

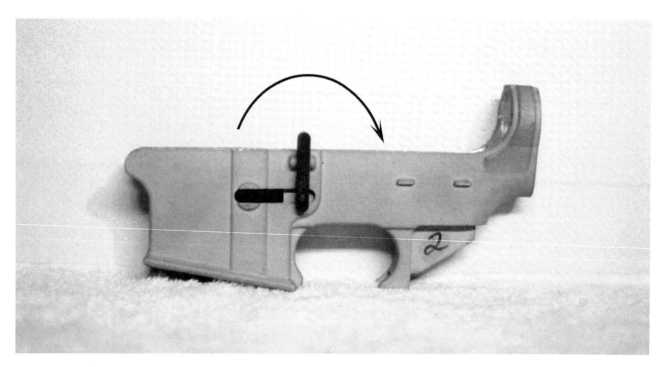

Figure 59. Pushing the magazine catch button in will allow the catch itself to clear the side of the receiver. It can then be turned clockwise to tighten it.

Place the spring onto the threaded end of the catch from the other side and screw the magazine button onto the threaded end a few turns. Depress the magazine button as far as you can into the well and turn the catch itself clockwise to tighten (Fig. 59) until it contacts the bolt hold-open pin housing. This is where you can scratch the receiver if you turn it too far. Release the button, and the catch should retreat into the recess. Insert a magazine and check the function of the magazine release. If it falls freely, then you are ready to install your fire-control parts.

Fire-Control Parts

Place the selector into the hole first, then your trigger (with the disconnector and disconnector spring in it this time). The hook on top of the disconnector needs to be facing forward (Fig. 60) so that the notch on the bottom seats onto the spring. Insert one of the hammer/trigger pins smooth end first (it doesn't matter which side you insert from) and wiggle the trigger and disconnector slightly as you try to work the pin through. This can take several minutes and become quite frustrating, so take your time. Once in place, the trigger will now keep the selector from falling out.

The hammer can be a little tricky to place in position because of the spring you are fighting while inserting the pin. The legs of the spring rest on the sides of the trigger, and you need to

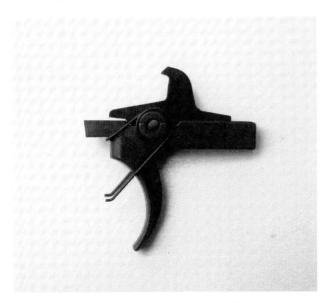

Figure 60. This is how the trigger parts will fit together inside the receiver.

hold the hammer down while lining it up. This takes practice. Note that the hammer can easily slip out and fly up at this point, so be sure to wear eye protection.

Once the hammer is in place, cock it and dry-fire with your hand over the hammer to prevent it from striking the casting. It should still work properly.

Pistol Grip and Selector Detent

Put the washer on the grip screw and place it through the hole in the grip. You will find this much easier to accomplish if you use a magnetized screwdriver. Place the selector detent (pointed end first) and the spring in the hole in the pistol grip. Carefully slide the grip onto the web and line the spring up with the hole in the receiver prior to tightening the grip screw.

Check the function of the selector by cocking the hammer and rotating the selector. It should click into both the fire and safe positions and should not move past either position. In the safe position, the trigger should not pull and the hammer should not release. Move the selector to the fire position and dry-fire with your hand over the hammer to avoid damaging the casting. Once fired, the selector should not be able to rotate back to the safe position until the hammer is cocked again.

Bolt Hold-Open Catch

Insert your bolt catch pin through the right ear of the housing so that it is ready to tap through the rest of the way when your parts are in place. This requires some know-how, since a roll pin is basically a roll spring—it must be compressed before you can install it. If it causes too many problems, use the six-penny nail instead. Place the spring in the hole and drop the buffer onto the spring so that the little end fits into the spring itself. Place the catch in the receiver and gently tap the pin into place through the hole in the catch and into the left ear of the housing. Check to see that the catch releases when you push on it.

Buffer Assembly,
Takedown Detent, and Butt Stock

Thread the buffer tube until it reaches the detent hole behind the fire-control pocket. Place the spring in the hole and drop the buffer detent over the spring. Push it down with your thumb and

Figure 61. Using the sander to remove material from the rear of the casting.

finish threading the buffer tube until it is tight. The front of the tube might press against the detent, causing it to lock in place. If this occurs, you will need to remove the tube and file some material from the end. *Be careful to hold the detent with your thumb as you unscrew the buffer tube* or the spring and detent will fly out and most likely be lost.

It is also possible that the tube will not quite reach the buffer detent. This is because the castings have extra material at the rear for "play." Remove some of this material with a floor-mounted belt sander (Fig. 61), taking care not to remove too much material. Be sure to keep it square! If you don't have access to a floor-mounted belt sander, an acceptable alternative is to use a medium/coarse file. Again, be certain to keep the surface flat and square in both directions.

Once your tube fits without interfering with the function of the detent, lock it into place with a wrench on the rear lug of the tube. Your buffer tube might be slightly crooked at this point even though you threaded the receiver properly. This is because the rear of the casting may not be perfect. See which way the tube needs to be straightened, then use the floor-mounted sander to change the plane slightly.

Slide your takedown detent and spring into the hole (if you have opted to use it) and slide the stock onto the tube. Secure it with the drain screw (it has a hole in it) using a large, flathead screwdriver.

Cock the hammer and slide the buffer spring and buffer into the buffer tube past the detent. The detent should then pop up and hold the buffer assembly in place.

Trigger Guard

Slide the front of the trigger guard into the receiver until the detent snaps into place and the rear hole aligns with the holes in the rear housing. Place a block of wood under this area when tapping your pin through, as you can very easily snap one of the flanges if you aren't careful!

Pivot Pin Detent

This can be a difficult installation, which is why I have saved it for last. It is best attempted with the aid of a pivot installation tool (available from Brownells) or very carefully with a thin-

Figure 62. This is the moment you have been waiting for! All your lower needs now is an upper and it is ready to fire. It can be left as is or finished for a more professional appearance.

bladed screwdriver. The spring and detent can launch from the hole like a missile if your hand slips, so be careful. This is especially true if you are using a screwdriver in lieu of the tool.

The installation tool is recommended if you are going to be building two or more rifles. If using one, align the hole in the tool (which looks like a round Allen wrench with a hole through it) with the detent hole in the front of the receiver. Drop the spring and detent into the detent hole and push down with a $\frac{3}{32}$ inch punch or a finishing nail.

Carefully rotate the tool so that the detent pops back up against it. You can now remove the punch or nail. Carefully slide the pivot pin in with the round portion touching the detent until it pushes the installation tool out of the way. Rotate the pin until the detent pops into the groove. The pin is now installed.

If you do not have an installation tool, hold the spring and detent in place with a small, flat-bladed screwdriver (like the type you use for repairing eyeglasses) and slide the pin in. Again, take care to avoid letting the screwdriver slip off the compressed parts or you may never find them. Once in place, the pin should not be able to be removed from the lower.

Your homebuilt lower receiver is now complete (Fig. 62).

To install your upper to your completed lower, slide your takedown and pivot pins out of the way, place the pivot lug of the upper into position, and pin it in place. Close the upper and secure it with the takedown pin. There is a slight chance that the bolt carrier will catch on the hammer when trying to close your AR-15. If this happens, simply cock the hammer and close the upper. Your AR-15 is now assembled and ready to test-fire.

TESTING AND FIRING

4

CAUTION

Before firing your rifle, be sure there is no oil in the bore! After firing and cleaning, it is common (and proper) procedure to oil the bore for storage. This is fine, but you should run a dry patch down the barrel prior to firing again. If there is excess oil in the bore of your firearm, it can result in reduced accuracy due to microscopic bore expansions. Also, always make certain that there are no obstructions in the barrel, such as dirt, squibs, or mud wasp larvae. (Yes, I have seen this. It takes only one afternoon of lying on the workbench.)

Now that your rifle is assembled, you will need to test it prior to firing. Cycle the action by hand to make sure the bolt carrier isn't sticking inside the buffer tube. Dry-fire it several times (it won't hurt it) to ensure that nothing hangs up or otherwise seems out of the ordinary. If you have purchased a commercial upper, then the headspace should be properly adjusted, and it should have been test-fired already at the factory.

Now is the time to play with all the little things that make the rifle work, including the selector, magazine release, and action. If all seems satisfactory, then it is time to take it to the range or sandpit for test firing.

All firearm safety rules apply! Always point the rifle in a safe direction and treat it as though it were loaded *at all times*. I have seen a supposedly empty AK-47 discharge through the roof at a check-in during a gun show. Fortunately, a fluorescent ceiling fixture was the only object killed in that particular moment of carelessness. Several months earlier, a girl had been shot in the face and killed by an "empty" handgun during a demonstration at another gun show. Even worse, the person responsible, a police officer, knew better. Yet he was certain the firearm was empty.

So again, never point your rifle at anything you don't intend to shoot, and always assume it's loaded. Never put your finger on the trigger until you are ready to shoot, and be sure you are firing into a safe backdrop that will not result in a dangerous ricochet or allow the bullet to pass through and unintentionally strike an object or person beyond. "An ounce of prevention is worth a pound of cure," my mother used to say. It applies here as well.

An important thing to interject here regarding .223 and 5.56mm: contrary to what others may tell you, there *is* a difference between the two. The .223 Remington is the cartridge that the 5.56mm cartridge was designed from, but the shoulder angle and cartridge neck are a few thousandths of an inch different. *Never* use 5.56mm ammunition in a rifle marked .223 (except for a Colt—those guns are marked .223 but are actually chambered in 5.56mm). A .223 round can be fired in a 5.56mm chamber because it is two thousandths of an inch shorter, but the longer 5.56mm cartridge may keep the bolt from closing in a .223 chamber, possibly blowing the gun up in your face! Many gun and ammunition dealers aren't even aware of this difference and will argue that they are one and the same. Trust me, they are not. If you have a .223 hunting rifle, *do not use military ammo in it.*

Now that you are ready to fire your new AR-15, start by donning adequate ear and eye protection and placing *one* round in the magazine. Chamber the round and fire the rifle. You may find that the brass doesn't extract—it may take a few shots to get the chamber polished. This is why I say to chamber only one round at a time at first. If this happens, break the rifle open, cock the bolt

back, and knock the cartridge out with a cleaning rod from the barrel end.

If it fires okay the first time or after the brass no longer sticks in the chamber, try two rounds. If that works to your satisfaction, fire five. If there are still no problems, then feel free to load the magazine and sight the upper in. The Bushmaster uppers I've used have all been right on the money, but those from other manufacturers may need sighting in. The A2 uppers are much easier to sight in, having adjustable windage and elevation knobs in place of the old, tool-adjusted sights of the earlier A1s.

At this point, if I am convinced the gun is safe and working to my satisfaction, I will usually rapid-fire several 30-round magazines in quick succession or a 120-round drum magazine. This will get the rifle good and hot, and if anything is going to work loose, it should do so by now.

After you've run through the first magazine, engage the safety and remove the mag. Carefully inspect all the pins to see if any appear to be working loose. If everything looks OK, then blow through the rest of the magazines and perform the same check. If anything has worked loose, or if you enlarged the hole too much in the drilling process, longer pins secured with e-clips are an option.

If everything looks satisfactory, cycle the action several times and dry-fire the rifle. Break it open and inspect the internal parts, checking for shavings or aluminum dust in the fire-control pocket. If everything still looks satisfactory, pat yourself on the back. You have successfully built your own AR-15 rifle.

FINISHES FOR YOUR LOWER

5

There are several methods you can use for putting a durable finish on your lower. The first, of course, is anodizing. Anodizing is a coating method that involves acid baths, electricity, and a dyeing process. You can anodize your lower yourself if you desire. The process isn't that complicated, but because of the sulfuric acid and electric current involved, it can be rather dangerous to perform. The acid can eat tissue rather rapidly, so getting it on your skin or, worse, in your eyes, may be a big dissuasion. In addition, the combination of electricity and sulfuric acid can produce highly explosive hydrogen gas. Even if you don't create enough gas to cause an explosion, it can still flash, causing severe burns and possibly setting your workshop on fire. If you must do your own anodizing, it is strongly advised that you perform the task outside or in a large, well-ventilated area. Do not attempt this procedure unless you are experienced with handling hazardous chemicals and know exactly what you are doing at all times.

Another option is to have your lower anodized professionally. Most companies charge a minimum of around $100, but if you will be making a few lowers, you can have them all anodized at once for the same amount of money as having each one done separately.

While there are some manufacturers that still anodize their AR-15 receivers, most are now using baked or epoxy finishes (some are even applying the finishes over the anodizing for an even greater effect). These receivers are a deep, rich black color as opposed to the purplish, grayish, or translucent black associated with anodizing. In addition to more uniform coloring, these new finishes are much more durable and scratch-resistant than anodizing, although some may not stand up to some of the "super solvents" on the market. For standard solvents, however, they hold up superbly, especially the epoxy finishes.

These finishes are available from Brownells and come in aerosol cans. Most are available in a variety of colors, so you can match your lower to almost any upper you purchase, or you can create custom camouflage patterns that won't wear off like spray paint. The baked finishes work well on metal; use the epoxy for your stocks, since you cannot put them in the oven.

Baking lacquer provides one of the most durable finishes. Available in several colors, it is highly resistant to oils, mild acids, and most solvents. It is sprayed on and baked in your oven at 325°F for 20 minutes.

Teflon/moly coating provides a durable finish that is resistant to friction. It is baked in your oven at 350°F for 30 minutes and is available in several colors as well.

Brownells' Gun-Kote is baked at 300°F for one hour and provides a tough, slick finish. It is available only in matte black.

Brownells also offers Aluma-Hyde II, a durable epoxy-based paint that withstands bore cleaners, solvents, and even trichloroethane. It is not a baked-on finish and will build up with additional layers, so it is not recommended for the inside of the lower, where your tolerances are close. It is ideal for stocks because it is recommended for both aluminum and plastic and does not need to be baked in the oven (which would melt plastic stocks and parts). It should not be sprayed on surfaces that tend to get very hot, such as barrels. It is available in several colors.

I recommend the baking lacquer for your lower, as it provides a tough yet easily applied finish and is probably the best all-around finish in terms of durability. In addition, should you choose to camouflage your rifle, it can be sprayed in a multicolored pattern that, upon baking, forms a single coat of camouflaged protection for your firearm.

It is entirely up to you whether to keep your AR-15 in military gray, finish it in civilian or spec-ops black, or camouflage it. If you make more than one, perhaps you can experiment and see which is more suited for your needs or tastes.

I hope you've had fun following the directions in this book to make your very own functioning AR-15 rifle out of an 80 percent finished lower receiver blank. It should give you years of shooting pleasure and one day may just save your life.

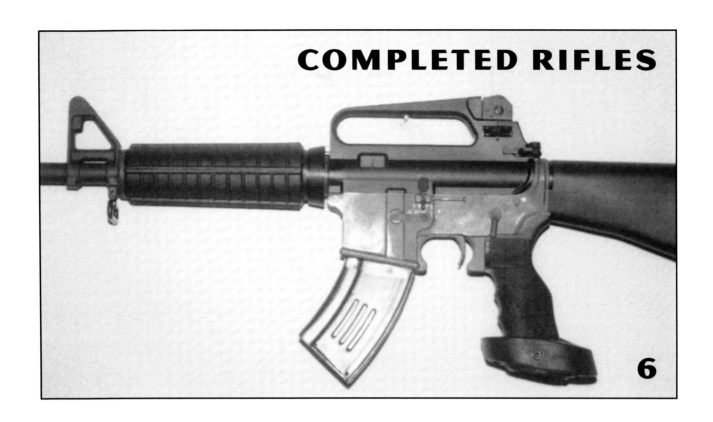

COMPLETED RIFLES

6

Here are a few of the rifles that I have built from scratch with 80 percent castings.

A 9mm built on an aluminum casting using a SOCOM Manufacturing conversion block.

A 5.56mm built on an aluminum casting.

A 7.62x39mm built on a copper/beryllium casting.

A .50 BMG built on an aluminum casting with a Ferret50 upper. It weighs in at only 25 pounds, but Cootie has no problem with the recoil.

Close-up of the .50 BMG receiver. Note that there is no selector or magazine catch assembly. The unique pivot and takedown pins came with the upper.

All addresses, telephone numbers, and Web addresses were current at the time of this book's publication. Telephone numbers change frequently, so they may no longer be in service in the future. Postal, Web site, and e-mail addresses tend to be more permanent. While many of these suppliers carry much more than is mentioned here, I am listing only parts pertinent to this project.

Bureau of Alcohol, Tobacco, Firearms,
   and Explosives
Office of Public and Governmental Affairs
650 Massachusetts Avenue, NW
Room 8290
Washington, D.C. 20226
www.atf.gov
(202) 927-7777

According to the ATF's Web site, the agency "cannot respond to e-mail inquiries relating to technical, policy, and/or legal questions. Inquiries of this nature can only be addressed through a letter outlining your questions" to the address above. You will receive a written response to your inquiry. The Web site provides e-mail addresses for specific questions about firearms ownership, manufacture, licensing, and related issues as well as an informative Frequently Asked Questions (FAQ) section.

Brownells
200 Front Street
Montezuma, IA 50171
www.brownells.com
(800) 741-0015

Source for AR-15 gunsmithing parts and tools, baking lacquer finishes, and more. Brownells caters to gunsmiths, so expect to pay for what you get. They do have some of the harder-to-find parts, such as the large-hole lower conversion pin.

DPMS/Panther Arms
3312 12th Street SE
St. Cloud, MN 56304
www.dpmsinc.com
(320) 258-4448

Supplier of most AR-15 parts.

Gun Parts Corporation
226 Williams Lane
West Hurley, NY 12491
www.gunpartscorp.com
(845) 679-4867
World's largest supplier of gun parts, including AR-15 parts kits and accessories.

National Ordnance
5850 San Felipe, Suite 500
Houston, TX 77057
www.nationalordnance.com
(713) 706-6205
Castings, forgings, jigs, drill bits, and many AR-15 parts.

Shotgun News
P.O. Box 1790
Peoria, IL 61656
www.shotgunnews.com
(800) 521-2885
Billing itself as "the world's largest gun sales publication," *Shotgun News* is a fine source for AR-15 cast and forged lower receivers and various upper receivers, plus almost anything you might need for your AR: parts, manuals, tools, ammunition, and more.

SOCOM Manufacturing
616 Atomic Road
North Augusta, GA 29841
www.socommfg.com
(803) 442-9206
Sells 9mm conversion blocks for Olympic Arms uppers only. These are the ones that will take unmodified Sten magazines.

AR-15 Plus
www.tar15plus.com
A one-stop shop for all your AR-15 build components: 80 percent lowers, lower parts kits, barreled upper receivers, drilling jigs, and tools.